MW01231817

# One Four Man Up

# One Four

# Man Up

## Robert E. Hunt

INFINITY
PUBLISHING.COM

Copyright © 2009 by Robert E. Hunt

*Cover design by Melissa Kennedy*

ISBN 0-7414-5210-3

*Published by:*

PUBLISHING.COM

*1094 New DeHaven Street, Suite 100*
*West Conshohocken, PA 19428-2713*
*Info@buybooksontheweb.com*
*www.buybooksontheweb.com*
*Toll-free (877) BUY BOOK*
*Local Phone (610) 941-9999*
*Fax (610) 941-9959*

*Printed in the United States of America*

*Printed on Recycled Paper*

*Published February 2009*

*To my loving wife, Peggy*
*...for her patience and understanding.*

*To my children, Jennifer and Melissa*
*...so that they may know their father better.*

*To the men I served with*
*...for getting me through it all.*

*The months others knew as youth, I spent learning the meaning of death.*

*The times others spent learning love, I passed hoping to live endless nights.*

*The moments others remember as laughs in classrooms, I remember as terror in the jungles.*

*The instants of pleasure taken for granted by others, I remember as forgotten hopes, long ago crushed by the reality of war.*

*The unfulfilled dreams of others are yet to be thought by me since I am in search of my elusive youth, looking for months lost in combat which are no more, and never will be.*

*Author Unknown*

# CONTENTS

# FOREWORD

This is the story of my tour of duty in Vietnam as a tactical air controlman and the effect it had on me afterwards. This is a true story told through my eyes and from my perspective. It has been over 40 years since I served my tour of duty there, so these events are based on my most vivid memories. Although I have researched the battles I fought in and the places I had been, these events are only as accurate as the information I could obtain and the memories I could recall.

Certain events in my life as well as circumstances at home led to my decision to join the Marines. My mother and I were not getting along well. I was not doing well in college and was not motivated to do so. College was something my parents wanted, not what I wanted. The war in Vietnam and fighting in that war were not even a consideration in my decision. I just wanted to get away from home.

It wasn't until a few years ago that I learned my mother had serious mental illnesses most of her life. I would always hear her say, "Oh, it's just nerves." I knew that she took a number of medications for "her nerves," but I never understood the gravity of her mental illness.

My mother suffers from narcissism, borderline personality disorder, and paranoid schizophrenia. These are very serious mental disorders that have a profound effect on her personality.

These illnesses existed in my mother at the time I decided to join the Marines and still exist today. Growing up with a mother who had such illnesses meant having to tolerate serious mental abuse. Lack of knowledge regarding them makes toleration almost impossible.

An understanding of her disorders would have changed everything in my life, so I would have to say that my mother was a deciding factor in why I joined the Marines. I felt that for my own mental health, I needed to get away from her influence. I needed to become my own person. I needed to become a man.

Another person who had an impact on me was my grandmother. I remember my grandmother often saying, "Bobby, you're my favorite grandson." I was her only grandson, but she said it in such a manner that it did not come across as a joke.

Even as a small child, my grandmother often talked about how I should someday become a Marine. She would say, "Bobby, someday when you grow up, you should join the Marines. They're the first to fight." Those words were still in my head the day I decided to take my grandmother's advice. This book chronicles the events that led up to my decision to join the Marines. The consequences of that decision are what made the events that followed worth writing about.

I know that a lot has been said and written about the war in Vietnam. There are history books, personal accounts, books on the military tactics of the war, books about the weapons used, books about anything and everything that has to do with the Vietnam War, so you're probably thinking that this book is going to be like so many others. I can assure you it isn't.

The experience of combat is traumatic. Ask any veteran of any war. We see war on TV, on the news, in the theaters, and we read about it in the newspaper. Since Vietnam, there has been U.S. military involvement in the Persian Gulf War, the invasion of Afghanistan, and most recently the Iraq War.

Whenever the United States gets involved in a war and soldiers are sent to fight, we soon become consumed by it all. The war in Iraq has been a part of our everyday lives for almost six years as of the writing of this book. The Vietnam War raged for ten years. By the time we had withdrawn from that war, the American people were fed up with it, and attitudes ranged from anger to apathy.

I believe that most people are good people with good intentions. I've seen support for our troops in Iraq and Afghanistan on bumper stickers, novelty items, Boy Scout and Girl Scout bake sales to benefit veterans, and investigative news reports to bring attention to injustices against our veterans.

I think that the events of 9/11 changed America in many ways. People are more patriotic; they fly flags, they shake your hand and thank you for your service to your country, they care about the veterans of the wars our country has chosen to fight.

However, in the late 60's, being a Vietnam veteran was not a good thing to be. When I returned home from my tour in Vietnam, there was no ticker tape parade, no bands playing, no girls jumping up and down in excitement to welcome me home. Basically, my return was disappointing.

It's probably difficult to imagine what it is like to step from an environment of being shot at and in constant fear to one of normalcy and routine, all in a matter of days. We take for granted, the transition of night to day and back to night, a routine of our lives that just is. So it stands to reason that the American people would take for granted the transition of everyday Joe to war veteran and back to everyday Joe.

When I returned from Vietnam, no one told me about Post Traumatic Stress Disorder, PTSD. No one told me about the recurring thoughts and anguish I would suffer for many long years after my return to "normalcy."

The year was 1969. People were protesting the war in front of the White House. Vietnam veterans were protesting the war. It was on the news every night, and it consumed the American people. So it is no wonder that no one wanted to hear about my experiences in the war. They just wanted it to end. Their intentions were good – bring our boys home, stop the death and maiming and destruction. We had no business being there in the first place. Sounds familiar even today.

But for me, it was important to talk about my experiences – the horrors I had witnessed, the extreme difficulties I endured. I'm sure you've heard the term "shell shock" from previous wars. That phrase was coined during World War I. I believe society completely overlooked the true meaning of that phrase during the Vietnam War. As a result, I and many Vietnam veterans paid a price. I found out all too quickly after my return that talking about my experiences was not a good thing.

I had been discharged from the Marines in September, 1969, three months before my enlistment ended so that I could attend college. I had returned from Vietnam on May 19, 1969.

Having grown up in Norfolk, Virginia, I returned home to attend college at Old Dominion University, then called Old Dominion College. This was my second attempt at getting a college degree. I had only been in classes for a week when an incident occurred that would cause me to withdraw from society and cease to talk about the war I had just survived. It would take another incident 20 years later to break the shell I had lived in and start the true healing process.

This book tells the story of my journey from a teenage boy to U.S. Marine, from Marine to combat veteran, and from combat veteran to civilian life as an adult. It was after that journey that I began a new journey of healing as I searched for resolution and answers to my experiences in the war. That journey has had a lasting effect on my adult life and has helped to shape me into the man, the husband, the father, the ex-Marine, and the combat veteran that I am today.

I've often heard the expression, "War is hell." Well, it is and I survived. What I didn't realize was the hell I would have to endure after I returned from the war. That was a different kind of hell.

# CHAPTER

## *ONE*

### THEY'LL MAKE A MAN OF HIM

I was 18 years old when I joined the Marines in November of 1966. After graduating from high school in June, I worked in construction during the summer months, building garages and room additions on houses for minimum wage, $1.25 an hour.

My parents wanted me to go to college, to get an education, and earn a good living. I guess that's what all parents want for their kids. I had enrolled at Old Dominion College in Norfolk, Virginia where we lived and I had grown up; but in the back of my mind I knew that college wasn't for me. I had barely graduated from high school; and, had it not been for summer school, I probably would have graduated a year later. My parents wanted me to become an engineer. Why, I'll never know. I really didn't know what I wanted to do with my life, but I did know that I didn't want to be an engineer. At the time, the only thing I knew for certain was that I wanted to get as far away from my mother and from home as I could.

My mother remarried when I was eight years old after divorcing my real father, Robert Campbell. He had deserted us and moved to Florida years earlier. My stepfather, William Carl Hunt, had adopted me and my younger sister, Pam, thus changing our name from Campbell to Hunt.

Our stepfather was a good man, kind and caring, but not what most kids would call a real dad; we were never that close. I enjoyed many outdoor activities – playing ball, fishing, camping, swimming and Boy Scouts, but he never participated in any of these activities with me. However, he became my role model as I grew up. He set an example of honesty, hard work, and self respect.

My mother, on the other hand, just wanted me out of the house and out of her hair. As an adolescent, life at home had grown troublesome for me. There was something wrong with me or something wrong with her. I couldn't really figure it out, but I was always getting into trouble with her and being yelled at for one reason or another. I just couldn't seem to please her no matter what I did.

My sister was nearly five years younger than I. She was still in junior high at the time; and due to our age difference, we were not very close. I remember she had many bouts with my mother as well.

Yes, my teenage years were tough. I was the runt of the neighborhood, always getting bullied and picked on by some of the bigger kids. I was thin, small, and below average in many respects, both physically as well as in school. It was a frustrating time.

When I started college, I went part time because my SAT scores were so low. I was not sure what I wanted to be, what career path I should pursue – my mother had made that decision for me. I knew very little about the war in Vietnam.

I had no interest in politics or much else going on in the world. I spent most of my days at the college pool hall instead of attending classes, and my grades were suffering as a result. I was eager to become a man, eager to experience life and seek adventure; but I had no idea of how I was going to do that. I felt like I was in a real rut. I saw no future for myself. Even though I had reached adulthood from the technical standpoint, my mother continued to treat me as a kid, "...as long as you're living in my house, you'll do as I say, I'm the mother, you're the son...."

As I look back at the events that led up to my enlistment, I can't really pinpoint what the argument with my mother was about. You could say the sky is blue, and she'd find some reason to disagree with you and argue the point. Nothing seemed to please her, and it could have been the most trivial of events that sparked it all. The fact of the matter is, I didn't care. I had reached my limit of mental abuse from her that day, and I ran out the front door and slammed it so hard the glass broke.

I was steaming with anger, and jumped into my car and sped away determined to get as far away from my mother as possible – permanently. I drove to my girlfriend's house to talk to her, but she wasn't home. So for a while, I just drove around trying to think of a way to leave home. I knew I needed money, a place to live, a way to support myself. At that moment it occurred to me – the military. That might be the answer.

My first inclination was to join the Air Force, to fly in planes or maybe even fly one myself. But the recruiter said they were full, and he couldn't enlist me at that time. He suggested the Navy.

Norfolk is a Navy town. Growing up, I had seen the Navy up close for many years; and it was not a branch of the service I would even consider. Don't ask me why, it just wasn't what I was looking for at the time.

The Air Force recruiter then suggested the Army. For some reason, I didn't have much respect for the Army either. I'd heard the term "doggies" used to describe Army personnel and it seemed a bit degrading to me. I think the term came from World War II, dog-faced soldier or something like that. So I politely declined that suggestion as well.

That left only two other branches of service to consider, the Coast Guard or the Marines. The Coast Guard was just another branch of the Navy, so that was out. The Marines, well, they were still a branch of the Navy; but I remembered the comments my grandmother had made to me, "Join the Marines, they're the first to fight." I remembered the uniforms were neat, those dress blues, and I knew the Marines were the most elite fighting force in the world. That was enough for me.

The Air Force recruiter directed me around the corner to the Marine Corps recruiting office on Grandby Street, and I immediately went in. I told the Sergeant I wanted to join.

First, they asked me how old I was. "Eighteen sir." They gave me some papers to fill out, last name first, first name, middle initial, that sort of thing. I took some tests and passed those with flying colors. (Maybe I did learn something in high school after all.) There was no mention of Vietnam, but the Sergeant did say I'd go through boot camp at Parris Island, South Carolina. My test scores were good enough to do most any job the Marines had to offer, but I wasn't given a choice of jobs; they'd choose just the right job for me when I graduated from boot camp.

I was excited. I had found a solution to my problem. I signed the papers. I was an adult. I didn't need anyone's permission, especially my mothers. My parents couldn't stop me; and, besides, it was too late now. I didn't care where they sent me, just as long as it was far from Norfolk, Virginia. I wanted adventure, glory, respect. Fighting in the war in Vietnam never even entered my mind.

I drove back to my girlfriend's house and found that she was babysitting for a neighbor down the street. I ended up spending the night at the neighbor's house and dreading going back to my parents and breaking the news to them.

My mother reacted as expected; it was just another argument, another one of her tantrums. I remember my stepfather saying, "They'll make a man of him...," and that's about all I can remember. I felt sorry for my younger sister, though. I would soon be free from my mother's control, but it would be many more years before Pam could break free.

I spent the next few weeks away from home as often as possible either at college, in the pool hall, or at my girlfriend's house. I left for Parris Island on December 1, 1966.

My adventure began with a bus ride to Richmond, Virginia where I was sworn in, had some last minute medical checks, signed some more papers, and waited to board a train for Parris Island. I made new friends, and we talked about what boot camp was going to be like. One guy got some beers, and we drank them in an alley near the train station as we waited.

The train ride lasted all night, and none of us slept much. We spent time memorizing our general orders which were in some of the paperwork we were given to carry with us. We arrived at the island around 10:00 a.m. the next morning, after being transported by bus from the train station in Beaufort, South Carolina. And so it began, a new life, new experiences, the transition from "boy" to "man."

"Get off the damn bus, NOW, you turds! Move it, move it, move it! What are you looking at, turd, don't you eyeball me."

"Sir, yes sir!"

"I can't hear you!"

An incredible hulk of a drill instructor (DI) had just welcomed us to Parris Island. We formed up on footprints painted on the asphalt. A number of DI's shouted obscenities at us, got in our faces, and did everything they could to intimidate and scare the hell out of us. It certainly worked.

We were then paraded into an old barracks that looked like a leftover from World War II days. The DI continued to spout obscenities about our mothers and "Jodie," that fictitious character who would be seeing our girlfriend while we were away. He demoralized and degraded us. We were pushed and shoved and yelled at as we were directed to strip down to our skivvies before being herded into a makeshift barber shop in the adjoining latrine (or "head" as it was called by the Marine Corps).

The head usually consisted of three rooms. There was a shower room which contained six to ten shower heads. There was a toilet room which contained the same number of urinals. The toilets sat in the open without stalls or privacy; and there was a sink room with six to ten sinks and mirrors for shaving, washing, and brushing teeth.

As I later understood, the object of this intimidation was to strip away our personal identity so that the Marine Corps could then begin the task of rebuilding us to their traditional standards of self-disciplined men. Self-discipline entailed many things. Self-discipline meant that you could do things required of you without supervision and without complaints. For example, a self-disciplined Marine in a combat environment could endure the intense heat of Vietnam all day, walk for miles with heavy equipment on his back, and go without water all day without complaints. He could endure things a common civilian could not, because he had been trained to do so and was expected to do so.

Soon, I was asking, "What in the hell had I gotten myself into?" This was totally unreal. Within minutes, our hair was gone (not that I had much to begin with). We were herded from one building to another being issued all kinds of military equipment, uniforms, underwear, personal hygiene items, a bucket, duffle bag, laundry bag. The load we had to carry got heavier and heavier. I weighed only 125 pounds to begin with, and the load I was issued to carry was at least that heavy itself. Every time I dropped something, the verbal abuse would start up again. How was I ever going to get through this mess? I had gone from the frying pan into the fire. My mother was tame compared to this.

We were given a quick meal at the "mess hall," which got its name quite appropriately from the cuisine served to us and the manner in which it was served. We were required to eat every particle of food placed on our metal trays, whether it was something we liked or not; and we had only minutes to scarf it all down. The different foods weren't separated but were basically all piled together in one big heap. I quickly learned not to put my tray out to the KP's for every item on the menu.

I made my first mistake later that day when we were given temporary sleeping quarters in yet another rickety wooden barracks. A drill instructor asked me some insignificant question and I replied with an answer that was unimpressive to him. To make matters worse, I called the warden of fear and intimidation a "DI" instead of the dignified title those letters stood for. I had just earned myself the distinct privilege of polishing a very large, metal garbage can, inside and out, with brass cleaner – senseless punishment that clearly fit the crime.

Until enough men had arrived to form a platoon, our training was put on hold. For the next several days, we went through meaningless routines cleaning and polishing anything that even remotely might carry a shine.

By the end of the second day, I had nearly lost my voice because we were constantly required to yell, "Sir, aye aye sir" at the top of our lungs. Every instruction given to us by the drill instructor required this enthusiastic response.

By day 3, our platoon was formed and we were moved into a new barracks that would become home to us for the next eight weeks. That first night in the new barracks as a full platoon was a memorable one. After enduring a day of constant verbal and physical abuse, endless hours standing at the position of attention, marching, physical training, lecturing, and other forms of seemingly meaningless harassment, we were given 30 minutes of "free time" to shave, shower, and write letters home.

Three of us stepped into the community style shower together and turned on the water. It was absolutely ice cold; there was no hot water whatsoever.

We began shouting in agony, making comments appropriate for such a surprising situation. We jumped in and out of the spray of water trying to acclimate our bodies to the cold temperature.

"Oooohhhh shit, it's cold! Damn it's cold!"

Suddenly and unexpectedly, a DI appeared in the doorway of the shower with a bucket in one hand. We all knew that we must be in some kind of trouble, just by his presence, but did not anticipate what was to come next.

Without warning, the DI raised the bucket and let loose its contents – icy, muddy swamp water. Now, we were covered with this freezing, stinking mess; and he began cursing and yelling at us to get out of the shower. Of course, we obeyed his command, fearing the consequences had we tried to argue with him. I wiped myself off with the towel I had been issued and slipped quickly past the DI and back to my bunk.

When free time ended, everyone was still mulling around, writing letters and such. Gunnery Sergeant Day, the senior drill instructor, stepped into the doorway of the barracks as silence fell upon the room.

"What do you turds think you're doing? Why isn't my barracks clean? Are you ladies having fun? Platoon, aaaaatttennntion!"

We snapped to attention as we had been taught to do earlier, standing in place in front of our bunks.

"Pick up those foot lockers, NOW!"

We picked up the foot locker that had been issued to us which now contained all of our uniforms and personal items. These were large, wooden boxes, approximately 3 feet by 2 feet by 2 feet; and they weighed every bit of 50 pounds, if not more.

"Get those damn foot lockers up! I want 'em chest high! Move it, move it turds!"

Sergeant Day stomped through the barracks yelling at the top of his lungs, madder than hell, and singling out the weaker men like me, who were having difficulty lifting the heavy lockers. He threatened us with all sorts of consequences if we disobeyed his order.

We were made to stand at attention, foot lockers held chest high, for 10 or 15 minutes until every single man had collapsed from exhaustion and could not hold the foot locker up any longer. Our weak, unfit muscles ached from the tormenting pressure. Every man in that barracks wanted to obey and please the drill instructor. No one wanted to quit, but the physical demands were just too much for any of us to bear. One by one, the lockers dropped to the floor. This, of course, only brought on more shouting, more threats, and more obscenities from Sergeant Day.

"What's the matter, are you ladies tired? So we've got a bunch of pussies, non-hackers in this platoon, huh? What about my barracks? Why isn't my barracks clean? Hit the deck turds, move it! I want you turds at attention on my deck, NOW!"

We obeyed his command and lay down on the floor wherever we could find space, as foot lockers littered the floor all around us. One by one, we snapped to attention, there on the floor, staring up at the lights hanging from the ceiling.

"Now, roll ladies, roll. Roll around on my deck until it's clean. You ladies want to play games, have fun? I'll teach you what fun is. You're in the Marine Corps now; this ain't your momma's house. This is MY barracks, and it WILL be clean!"

So we rolled, from side to side, in our Marine Corps skivvies (boxer shorts and a T-shirt) for five or ten minutes, mopping the floor with our bodies. Was this ridiculous or what? Was this meaningful or what? How was this little exercise going to prepare us for war?

"On your feet turds, on your feet! Platoon, aaaattennntion!"

So we jumped to our feet and snapped to attention once again, standing in our assigned positions in front of our bunks. Our bunks were metal bunk beds, two men to a bunk. My bunk was on the bottom. As we stared straight ahead into deep space, no one dared to bat an eyelash.

Sergeant Day walked slowly down the center of the room, pushing foot lockers aside and out of his path, his arms behind his back, eyeing each and every one of us, just waiting for someone to screw up, to eyeball him.

"What are you looking at, turd? Are you eyeballing me boy? Don't you eyeball me, turd! I'll rip those suckers right out of your head!"

The Marine Corps' position of attention required that you keep your head and eyes forward at all times, looking nowhere. Never were you permitted to make eye contact with the drill instructor. Even if he came right up into your face, you were not permitted to look him in the eyes. You could look at his chin, look at his lips, look at the hairs growing out of his nose, but you could not look him in the eyes. If you did so, you brought the wrath of God down upon yourself.

"Get down and give me 20! Now turd!"

"Give me 20" would become familiar words in the weeks to come – 20 pushups. We would find ourselves pushing the earth so much in the days to come, it's no wonder we didn't push the earth clean out of its orbit.

"Sir, aye aye sir!"

The recruit obeyed, dropped immediately to the floor, and began pushing the floor as he counted off loudly, "One sir, two sir, three sir…"

"Prepare to mount!"

"Sir, prepare to mount, aye aye sir." Our response was loud and in unison, but not loud enough.

"I can't hear youuuuuu!" the DI shouted.

"Sir, prepare to mount, aye aye sirrrrr!" we quickly responded.

"I still can't hear you!"

"SSIIIRRR, PREEEEPARRRRE TOOO MOOOUNT!, AAAYYYEEEE AAAYYYYEEEE SIIIRRRR!" we yelled once again, straining every muscle in our throats and lungs to please the DI.

As we had been taught earlier that day, we took one step aside and two steps backwards positioning ourselves at the side of our bunks. One man went left, one man went right. We remained at the position of attention looking across at each other and waiting for the next command.

"Mount!"

"Sir, mount, aye aye sir!"

We quickly pulled back the covers and crawled into our bunks, resuming the position of attention in our beds.

"Sleep!"

This required no response as the lights went out and all was quiet and calm for now. Sergeant Day left the room.

The next day, we faced a rude but routine awakening at 4:00 a.m. Bright lights came on as the duty drill instructor walked through the barracks banging a night stick against the lid of a large metal garbage can.

"Get up! Get up! Get out of the rack! Move it, you maggots! Reveille! Reveille!"

We jumped from our bunks and came to the position of attention in front of them, as we had been taught to do the day before.

"Platoon 125, count off!" the DI shouted.

"One, two, three…"

This was another daily routine that we had been taught. The purpose was to account for everyone in the platoon in a quick and efficient manner. Each man was assigned a number. The head count was to ensure that no one had gone AWOL during the night. Odd numbers were on the bottom bunk; even numbers were on the top bunk. I was an odd number.

"Get this barracks straight! Now, ladies! We ain't got all day! Formation in five minutes. Move it!"

We had five minutes to get dressed, straighten our foot lockers, make our beds, and get outside with our M-14 rifles and field pack. Every day, the first event required us to run two miles wearing combat boots and fatigues and carrying combat gear which consisted of a 16 pound weapon and a 10 pound pack.

And so it began – eight weeks of Marine Corps boot camp. Over the next eight weeks, our bodies and our minds would be pushed to the limits, further than we could imagine. Most would consider the things we learned to endure routinely sheer torture. But it was just the beginning of the process of molding raw civilian boys into United States Marines and combat soldiers. We would learn to work as a team, not as individuals.

We spent countless hours each day, marching in drill team fashion around a parade ground the size of a small airport runway. It never seemed to fail that someone would "fuck up"; but rather than punish the single man, the entire platoon would be punished with pushups or PT. We learned to take verbal abuse in stride, including intimidation, threats, and obscenities.

We ran what seemed like endless miles, marched countless steps, stood at attention for an infinite number of hours, in addition to the physical training, the military classes on weapon assembly and disassembly, on Marine Corps regulations, and on combat tactics and related issues.

The Marine Corps had also developed certain routines that seem ridiculous to most civilians. For example, those who smoked were permitted to do so, but only three times a day, once after each meal. To smoke, you had to stand in a circle on the assembly area beside the barracks, cigarette in hand, and at the position of attention. "The smoking lamp is lit," the DI would shout. "Sir, the smoking lamp is lit, aye aye, sir!" the men would respond.

They were given five minutes to smoke their cigarettes before the command was given, "The smoking lamp is out!" The men would reply, "Sir, the smoking lamp is out, aye aye sir!"

At that command, the recruits were required to roll the remaining portion of the cigarette between their thumb and forefinger until the burning portion and any remaining tobacco had dropped off leaving only the filter. This was called "field stripping." Then, an assigned recruit would carry a bucket around the circle; and each smoker would place his butt in the bucket.

Another disciplinary measure used upon us was a rule about talking. During our entire training period, we were not permitted to talk to another recruit; and we could only talk to the drill instructor if we requested and obtained permission to do so. Of course, we took advantage of every moment alone to violate this rule so we could be brought up to date on the latest "scuttlebutt" going around.

This policy of not speaking without permission was where I made my second big mistake during that eight week period of pure hell. One day, the drill instructor had us assemble in a circle while he threw out questions on military courtesy and other such matters. I found that I knew very few of the answers and feared that he would call on me to answer one. I knew what would happen if I didn't know the answer.

Finally, a question was asked that I did know the answer to. In my haste to show my knowledge, I blurted out the answer before being called upon to do so. As if that weren't enough, I did so without even asking permission to speak to the drill instructor. This was the ultimate "kiss of death."

Fuming with anger for disrupting the class, the DI ordered me to go to the head and do 1000 bends and thrusts – an exercise that was torture to all the muscles in your body. To ensure that I obeyed his command, he also instructed the largest man in the platoon to accompany me. This recruit could have easily played linebacker for a professional football team. He was instructed that, for every repetition of the exercise that I did not do, he would have to do one.

I was determined to carry out my orders just to prove myself worthy of becoming a Marine. I don't know how much time had elapsed, but when the drill instructor came into the head to see if I was obeying his command, I had completed over 600 repetitions.

"How many have you done turd?"

"Sir, 623, sir!" I shouted as I continued to perform the exercise.

"Get out, maggot, NOW!"

"Sir, aye aye, sir!"

As I look back on that event today, I know the point that the drill instructor was trying to make was self-discipline. The Marine Corps wants you to do exactly what you are told to do, by people who know. Nothing more and nothing less is expected of you. This requires self-discipline without question. It was a concept drilled into our heads daily and in many different ways. It was also a concept that would later prove to be a life saver when the going got tough.

We spent much of our free time standing at the position of attention in front of our bunks while studying the Marine Corps manual, a guide to weapons, drill, history, and the *Esprit de Corps* tradition for which the Marine Corps was known. Quite often nature called and a recruit had the need to relieve himself; but you were not permitted to do so without first obtaining permission.

"Sir, Private Hunt requests permission to speak to the drill instructor, sir!"

"Speak, turd."

"Sir, the Private requests permission to make a head call, sir!"

Normally, after each meal, the drill instructor would announce "head call" as we stood at attention in front of our bunks.

"Port side, make a head call."

"Sir, port side make a head call, aye aye sir!"

"Bullshit, I can't hear you. Starboard side, make a head call!"

"Sir, starboard side make a head call, aye aye, sir!"

The barracks was divided at the center by a doorway that led into the head. Facing the door, the left side of the barracks was called the "port side" and the right side of the barracks was called the "starboard side." (These were Navy terms because the Marine Corps was originally born out of the Navy.)

When the order was given, the two sides would yell out the expected response competing to see which side could shout the loudest. I think it was all just one of those games the drill instructors liked to play with us because I could never tell the difference in intensity between the two sides. Inevitably one side would eventually be picked to go first.

"Starboard side, move it turds, move it!"

The designated men would then make a mad dash for the head doors. The first couple of days in our platoon barracks, it never seemed to fail that as soon as we got into the head, hurrying to relieve ourselves, the DI would be yelling at us to get out. It proved to be yet another one of those tortuous and agonizing routines, but we soon learned to control our bladders since there was not sufficient time to take care of the matter and meet the drill instructor's expectations! Self-discipline, what else could it be?

After completing half of our boot camp training, we were moved from our old World War II barracks to the rifle range and newer barracks. These barracks were equipped with larger, more modern facilities. There was actually hot water!

We spent two weeks at the rifle range. During the first week, we spent hour upon hour just holding our M-14 rifle in various fighting positions. These were positions we would be required to use when qualification week began. They called this first week "snap-in." The purpose of these exercises was to strengthen our muscles and get our bodies accustomed to the weight of the weapon. Snap-in was also another form of self-discipline. The rifle became extremely heavy after we stood like statues holding it in a particular position for over an hour. If you lowered or dropped the weapon from the snap-in position before the drill instructor told you to, the DI's almighty wrath would come down on you! Snap-in was grueling, tiring, and boring to say the least.

In the second week, qualification week, we began firing the weapon. The target was a large set of concentric circles with a 12 inch black bullseye. The target was made of heavy paper about 5 feet square mounted on a platform that could be hoisted up and down like a sail on a ship.

A large mound of dirt formed a small hill with a cement wall behind it where a crew of two men raised and lowered the target. Each time the shooter fired at the target, it was lowered; and a large button with a peg in it was inserted into the hole. Then, the target was raised back up. This allowed the shooter to see where his bullet hit and make adjustments to the sights on the weapon, if necessary, before he fired the next shot. The target would be lowered again and the button removed. The hole was then patched with a black or white square of paper similar to a postage stamp.

If the bullet struck the white area of the target, a black button was inserted into the hole. If the bullet struck the black bullseye, a white button was inserted. If the bullet missed the target completely, the pit crew would waive a red flag, commonly referred to as "Maggie's drawers," above the dirt mound. Each time the red flag was waived, you could rest assured the drill instructor was chastising the shooter regarding the consequences he would suffer if he failed to qualify.

At the end of the second week, we all had to qualify. Thursday was prequalification day and I had been shooting really well all week. Even at 500 yards, I was hitting the bullseye nearly every time. (At 500 yards, the bullseye was nothing more than a small black dot.) Often, my score at the end of a shooting round was nearly perfect. I was feeling pretty confident about my shooting and knew I would have no trouble qualifying as a rifle expert. I had found something I could do really well, considering I had never handled a real weapon prior to the Marine Corps.

On qualification day, I learned from some of the other men that several of the drill instructors had made bets against each other on what I would score. At the time, I was the top shooter in the platoon.

Though proud of myself, I felt somewhat uneasy about this situation. It placed a lot of pressure on my shoulders. Win or lose, some drill instructor would be pissed at me; and I'd never hear the end of it!

I shot well that day but missed the expert qualification by a few points and instead qualified as a rifle sharpshooter. Off day I guess, or was it? Still, I feared some form of repercussion from the losing DI.

I found out later what really went on that week. When we returned from the rifle range, the DI called two of the men into his office and closed the door. We could hear some intense vocal reprimands coming from the room. A few minutes later the men emerged. Both were doubled over and showed definite signs of having just experienced a painful lesson of some sort.

What I didn't know until graduation day was that these two men were the range pit crew for me during prequalification. The men had intentionally shown the bullet strikes near or in the bullseye even when the bullet had not struck there. In other words, they had cheated for me during pre-qualification making it appear that I was some whiz bang shooter, when I really wasn't. I guess, had I not qualified, I would have been given a second chance due to their interference. (It was very important to know where your bullets were hitting the target so that you could make windage adjustments to your weapon's sights.)

After rifle qualification, our training began to wind down. We spent the next two weeks pulling mess duty. Most of the men in the platoon worked in the mess hall, but I was fortunate. I was among a small few who were sent to work at the NCO barracks. This was a special barracks for non-commissioned officers who worked on the base. They had soda and candy machines in the barracks, and we were able to pig out when no one was around! It was a fun two weeks, to say the least!

The final week of training involved a long, ten-mile forced march with full equipment, knapsack, entrenching tool, weapon, magazines, canteens, the whole nine yards that typically we would carry on our bodies in a combat situation. We pitched tents, slept on the ground, and ate C-rations out of a can. It was sort of a final test of all we had learned, and morale was high because we all knew our boot training was coming to an end. We had endured; we had survived. For the first time in our short Marine Corps career, the word "survival" became meaningful and a serious word in our vocabulary.

During the eight weeks of boot camp training, we went through a number of specific milestones. One day, we spent hours at a desk taking all kinds of tests that would be used to determine our permanent MOS (Military Occupational Specialty), our job in the Corps. Part of the test involved learning a few Morse Code letters and then taking a brief Morse Code message. I did well on that test because I had learned Morse Code when I was a Boy Scout.

Another test that I did not do well on was the swimming test. This nearly killed me! We were required to jump into a swimming pool with water well over our heads. We were fully clothed in our fatigues, and we had to float in the water using a very special technique we were taught. Basically, you floated face down in the water. Every few seconds, you would do this special stroke with your hands and feet. It was to keep you from sinking to the bottom while you raised your head out of the water and took a breath of air. Then, your face went back down into the water. Supposedly, you could survive for hours on end without exerting much energy if you followed this procedure.

Well, I jumped into the pool and sank straight to the bottom! I panicked and began fighting desperately to get to the surface and breath. I could not catch my breath and relax because the weight of the wet fatigues pulled me under. I fought and fought to stay on the surface and tired very quickly, to the point that my body could no longer endure the strenuous muscle requirements. I sank to the bottom for one last time. The drill instructor had to fish me out of the pool, and I failed the test. Fortunately, so did many others. Apparently, it was not a test we were required to pass in order to graduate.

We also spent time at the hospital receiving all kinds of shots in the arm for what seemed like every disease known to man! It didn't occur to us that these inoculations were inevitably to protect us against diseases found in Vietnam.

Our photos were taken in dress blue uniforms which turned out to be only the front of the dress blue uniform tied in the back so that it would fit most anyone! (So much for those good looking uniforms that had enticed me into joining – I never did own a real set of dress blues.) A platoon photo was also taken, including the drill instructors.

We marched every day to learn the various drill moves and to enhance our self-discipline. We pulled guard duty, sat in classes listening to boring lectures, attended church on Sundays, and washed our fatigues and skivvies on a cement work stand with cold water, a scrub brush, and a bar of soap.

We polished our boots with saddle soap to keep them soft and were not allowed to use real shoe polish on them until final inspection. This was a very special inspection of our uniform and weapon just prior to graduation. Our weapons were intensely dirty after firing them at the rifle range; and we had to return them to their original, pristine condition. You can't even imagine the ingenuity of the drill instructor when it came to finding places for dirt and soot to hide in those weapons!

Then, there was the confidence course. I found this to be fun, but most didn't. When I was in the Boy Scouts, we had gone out into the woods one day and constructed a confidence course, but on a smaller scale. It consisted of rope ladders, tree ladders, inclined fallen tree walks, hurdles to jump, fallen trees to crawl under and that sort of thing. We'd run the course timing each other with a stop watch to see who could negotiate the different obstacles in the shortest amount of time. The Marine Corps' confidence course was similar in nature, only larger so I thought it was great fun. I wasn't the fastest to run the course, but at least I finished it. Not everyone did; some lacked the self-confidence to negotiate some of the obstacles.

On graduation day, we had finally earned the distinction of being called "Marine." It was a proud moment. We were no longer "turds" or "maggots." Gone were the days of verbal abuse. We had passed all of the tests, met the challenges thrown at us, and we had earned the respect of our drill instructors.

All of the challenges we had overcome had one main purpose, to prepare us physically as well as mentally for the ultimate challenge in our short lives, the challenge of surviving combat.

A few of the original men of Platoon 125 did not survive. Some were discharged altogether, while others were sent to "Motivation" platoons for an attitude change. They were given a second chance to prove their worthiness as United States Marines.

Graduation day reunited us with family members. My parents attended, and my high school sweetheart was there as well. It was a very proud day for us all as we marched past the bleachers and were congratulated by our Commanding Officer for having completed boot camp and for becoming

Marines. After the formal exercises of graduation, we were given the remainder of the day off as free time to spend with our families and show them around the base; but we were not permitted to leave the base. We had only completed the first phase of our training when we graduated from boot camp. There was still much more to come!

*Graduation Day with Evelyn*

At the end of the day we returned to the barracks and were assembled into a large circle. The senior drill instructor stood in the center of the circle and, one by one, called out each of our names and read out loud our new Marine Corps MOS, the job we would do upon completion of our training.

"Hunt."

"Here, sir."

"Twenty five thirty three, radio telegraph operator."

"Sir, aye aye, sir!"

Radio telegraph operator, that was to be my job in the Corps. I guess all that Morse Code I learned in the scouts had paid off, or had it? It sounded like a good job, a cushy job sitting at a radio and sending Morse Code or taking Morse Code messages. I had no idea what lay ahead of me.

PLATOON 125
FIRST RECRUIT BATTALION          M.C.R.D., PARRIS ISLAND, S.C.
SSGT. F.E. ALLEN    SSGT. C.W. DAY    SSGT. S.J. BARKER    SGT. K.J. KINNEY
GRADUATED 8 - FEB. - 1967

*Platoon 125, 1967*

CHAPTER

# *TWO*

## INFANTRY TRAINING

From Parris Island, we were shipped out the next day to Camp Geiger, North Carolina, a part of Camp Lejeune. We would spend the next three weeks or more learning combat techniques and tactics, infantry training. This was additional training that every Marine had to go through regardless of his MOS; because when the going got tough, you were a Marine rifleman, and regardless of your job, you had to know how to do one special job and do it well – fight in combat.

Infantry training would familiarize us with the various weapons used by the Corps in war. We would learn how to use them and how to maintain them. Combat tactics would also be new to us. We had already learned how to fire our M-14 rifles effectively, hitting a target as far away as 500 meters. Tactics were more than just firing the weapon. They were a set of procedures used by a fighting unit to achieve an objective, take a hill, secure a fighting position, that sort of thing. We would learn more about working as a team. Boot camp had only prepared us for individual tasks and responsibilities, such as keeping physically fit, knowing how to maintain and service our weapons, pitch a tent, cook C-rations. Now, we would learn how to pull together as a unit and work as a team to accomplish a mission.

I had thought that the worst was now behind me; we all did. Three weeks, piece of cake. That's all that was left before we could get our first leave and go home for a few weeks of rest and relaxation, R & R. I was eager to wear my uniform and show off the pride I had in my accomplishments, the pride of a Marine.

We arrived at Camp Geiger in February of 1967. It was a small base devoted strictly to the training of graduated recruits. The base was sort of desolate and dreary looking from the moment we passed through the gates.

Rows of one story, cinder block buildings lined the gravel roads – no grass, no flowers, and no statues of fighting Marines or memorials to honor the ancestry of the Corps. The base was no more than a few city blocks in size.

At one end was a drive-in theater with benches in place of the normal lot where cars could park. I wondered if we would get to go to the movies often. At the other end was the mess hall, a small PX (post exchange), a barber shop and a uniform store. The remainder of the base was surrounded by pine trees and a tall chain-link fence with barbed wire across the top. It sort of reminded me of a prison. It was the dead of winter, cold, with a very gray and dreary looking sky. A sort of surreal feeling came over me as we entered the base.

The bus pulled to a stop in front of a cinder block barracks where a sergeant stood waiting for our arrival. The door swung open, and the sergeant stepped aboard gazing down the aisle at his now captive audience.

"Okay Marines, I'm Sergeant Davis. I'm your platoon sergeant for the next few weeks here. I want a formation on the road. Answer up when I call your name and exit the bus. Anderson, John J."

"Here, sir!"

"Don't call me 'Sir' Marine! I'm a sergeant, I work for a living!"

Oh boy, here we go again. As the sergeant called our names, each answered with a loud "Here, sergeant" and scurried off of the bus and into formation. It seems the rules had suddenly changed. It had been drilled into our heads for eight weeks to always answer with the word "Sir" and now we're told something different!

The formation quickly filled and was called to attention once the last man had fallen in. Then, the order "At ease" was given as two more sergeants walked out of the barracks to join Sergeant Davis. Sergeant Davis introduced these men as instructors who would be part of our daily training during our stay here. He went over our basic training schedule which seemed rather routine. The atmosphere was much more casual than what we had encountered at Parris Island. But then again, we were Marines now, not low life scumbags just off the street! We had earned the respect of the sergeants now and they made no attempt to demoralize us as had been the case when we first arrived at the island.

As the sergeant spoke frankly and candidly about our training, for the first time the war in Vietnam was discussed. Emphasis was placed on the fact that Marines were dying every day in Vietnam and that some of those deaths were attributed to the personal failures of the men themselves. The sergeant emphasized that the Marine Corps tradition was teamwork, and we would learn more about applying that teamwork principle here at Camp Geiger.

This 15-minute lecture seemed a sort of pep talk and was already causing a sense of motivation to sweep through me. We were finally being treated with respect, spoken to frankly. This Vietnam War was serious business, your life was at stake. The talk made me feel more like a man than the boy I actually was. What lay ahead of us would require courage and fortitude that only a man could possess. At least, that was the sense I had from the sergeant's words. The sergeant talked about the generations of men before us who had fought on the beaches of Normandy in World War II and the Chosin Reservoir in the Korean War. Then, we heard about places like Con Tien, the Rockpile, and the DMZ. It all sounded mysterious but exciting, and I felt proud and honored to have been given this opportunity to fight for my country. By the time Sergeant Davis had finished his lecture, I was beaming with pride that I was a Marine and that I had endured basic training. I had survived and was convinced that I would survive the next few weeks of training as well.

Sergeant Davis also explained some of the camp rules. We could not leave the base; however, during our free time, we could go to the PX, see a movie in the outdoor theater, or just relax, write letters, or take a nap. Wow, this was different – freedom, no 24/7 baby sitter to watch our every move.

When the sergeant finished, our sea bags, which contained everything we owned, had been unloaded from the bus. Then, we were given the command to fall out, pick up our sea bags, and get settled in the barracks. We spent our first evening in the barracks unsupervised, and such freedom felt great. Lights out was at 9:00 p.m., but men talked in the dark well after that. This sort of made it difficult to go to sleep, but most of us were too excited to sleep anyway. There was a sense of relief that we were finally being called "Marine" and being treated so much differently than we had become accustomed to.

At 2:00 a.m., things changed. The fluorescent lights came on and sergeants entered the squad bay yelling at us.

"Reveille! Reveille! Let's go Marines, out of the rack, feet on the deck, let's go!"

We scurried to our feet and positioned ourselves at the front of our bunks snapping to attention. What time was it anyway? Seems like we just went to bed. I thought reveille was at 5:00 a.m., it can't be 5:00 a.m. already.

"What is this mess? Let's go Marines, we haven't got all day!" The sergeants started pulling mattresses off of the bunks and throwing them on the floor. Wall lockers at the front of the bunks were turned over and slammed to the floor.

"This place looks like a pig sty! Look at this barracks, what is this mess?"

In a matter of minutes, the quiet squad bay had turned into pandemonium with the yelling of sergeants and the banging of falling wall lockers, turned over beds, total confusion. It was chaotic.

"Get this barracks cleaned up, formation in 30 minutes. Let's move it Marines!"

We were all stunned by this sudden intrusion of our sleep and this new method of waking us. As quickly as they entered, the sergeants had disappeared leaving us all wondering what had just happened and even more than that, why?

"What the hell was that all about?" someone asked.

It didn't appear so obvious to us at the moment; but as I look back after all these years, I think that the point of this incident was quite clear and clever. The point was to give us our first real taste of the meaning of the word "teamwork." Our barracks was a mess; it looked like a tornado had hit it. We would have to work quickly to put it all back together. We would have to work as a team, not as a bunch of individuals. The wall lockers were too heavy for one individual to simply lift and put back in place. Surprisingly enough, we went right to work, as a team, cleaning up the mess before us, without supervision, without someone in charge to tell us exactly what to do next. It was like instinct. We all knew what had to be done; and we quickly set about doing it, helping each other, helping ourselves, helping our platoon. There was no bickering or fighting among ourselves.

After straightening the barracks, we were hustled outside into formation and marched to the mess hall. It was dark and cold, and I wished I had been able to sleep longer. I was afraid we were in for a very long day. We had to wonder, "What next?"

The food wasn't bad, better than it had been at the island. We were given about 30 minutes to eat as we sat at long picnic tables devouring the hot chow from our metal mess trays. After chow, we marched back to the barracks and stood in formation on the gravel road under the light of stark lamps on the telephone poles along the road.

Sergeant Davis explained our training schedule in detail now. For the next four weeks, we would be subjected to some of the most intense training exercises we could imagine. However, we would not start our actual training for a week. We were to pull KP (kitchen police) for the next seven days. What that meant was that we would work in the mess hall, helping the cooks out, cleaning things, dishing out the chow, that sort of thing. "Okay, no big deal, I can handle that," I thought; but the week that followed was a living nightmare. KP began at 3:00 a.m. every morning and ended around 10:00 p.m. at night. By the time we marched back to the barracks, took a shower and got ready for bed, it was nearing midnight. There was little time to sleep. To make matters even worse, our barracks or the head was usually destroyed when we arrived. We were awakened shortly after we hit the rack with this torturous routine of barracks destruction.

This all became a game. Before long, the sergeants were pitting us against other platoons in other barracks. They would take us on missions in the late night hours to destroy another barracks. It was unreal; it was pointless, or was it?

At that time, if asked, I would not have been able to describe the rationale behind that week of sleep deprivation and harassment. We were constantly busy, and we were constantly challenged and forced into team situations. The pitting of one barracks against another was an example of this.

By the time we had finished our week of KP hell, we were ready for more challenges; and we would get them. The infantry training that came next was a welcome relief, and the nightly harassment ended as quickly as it had begun. We were given ample time to rest our sore, tired bodies. We faced many physical and mental challenges. During the next three weeks, we walked an average of 12 miles a day to the firing ranges. We fired various weapons such as a machine gun, M-1 rifle, a rocket launcher, and even a flame thrower.

We set off a stick of dynamite, went on simulated patrols, and crawled under barbed wire while machine guns were fired three feet over our heads. We threw live hand grenades and felt our way through the dark for 20 meters in a simulated booby trap field. (Instead of explosives at the end of the trip wires, there were flares.)

Then there was the gas chamber – a sealed room with no windows, only an entry door on one side of the room and an exit door on the other side. The gas we were exposed to was not a lethal gas. It wouldn't kill you, but it would sure make you think that you were dying. It was tear gas.

When we entered the room, we were wearing a military issued gas mask that was designed to protect us not only from tear gas but also lethal gases known to exist in enemy arsenals. Our fatigues protected our bodies; and the mask protected our lives, or so we thought.

We had heard lots of rumors about the gas chamber and were extremely apprehensive about going through this part of our training. But nothing, absolutely nothing, could have prepared us for what we were about to encounter.

Upon entering the smoke-filled room, we were approached one-on-one by an instructor also wearing the same gas mask and fatigues. The instructor talked to us calmly and tried to reassure us that everything was okay. He asked "Are you okay, Marine?" and we replied accordingly.

He asked each of us our name, our serial number, our rank, and other routine questions, Even though we had a gas mask on, trying to breathe and answer these questions quickly became difficult. Though the mask filtered the gas, you knew it was present, you felt it on your skin, like a thousand needles pricking you; and you quickly began feeling it in your lungs as you began to gasp for air and answer the instructor's questions. Something was wrong. Was it supposed to burn and affect you like this when you're wearing a gas mask?

Then the worst part of the exercise came, you were instructed to take a deep breath and remove your mask. I thought fine, I can hold my breath for a minute or two. Surely I'll get to leave once I complete this part of the exercise.

The moment I removed the mask, the full extent of the gas took its intended effect immediately, and I panicked, as I'm sure every other Marine who had gone through this exercise had. My eyes were burning intensely. My skin was burning as the adrenaline rushed through my entire body.

The instructor started asking those same questions all over again. I could no longer hold my breath, I had to answer the questions. When I did, that first gulp of air sent indescribable pain through my entire body.

My lungs burned, and I was choking, gasping for air. I took in a big breath trying to get oxygen to my lungs which just made matters worse. The more I tried to gain my breath, the more gas I took into my lungs. I thought I was literally dying.

I could not breathe. Every attempt I made to get oxygen to my lungs only tormented me. My eyes were burning so badly that I couldn't keep them open. The instructor kept asking me those stupid questions, but I could not answer. I could only think about dying and that this was going to be the end.

Moments after the mask had been removed and I had been exposed to the full measure of the gas and felt its effect, I was whisked out of the room and into fresh air. Every pore in my body burned, I was choking, coughing, gasping for air. So was every man around me. It is difficult to describe just what this event was like. But it is one I surely will never forget, and one I surely do not want to experience ever again.

It took 15 minutes or more before I began to return to normal breathing and the pain began to subside. I had survived the gas chamber, and now I was feeling that I could survive anything they could throw at me. I felt that this had to be the worst of it, but there was still more training to come.

One training course we went through was a walk through a wooded area where there were silhouette targets that would pop up from behind trees and bushes. We had to crank off three shots from our M-1 rifles and knock the targets over. Sometimes you were right on the target without even seeing it, and it made me wonder if Vietnam would be this way (assuming of course, we went to Vietnam). Would our reflexes be keen enough to hit that live target in a real combat situation? It was scary to think that the next time we did this, that pop-up target would be a real human being who wanted to kill us.

The instructors talked often about combat situations and Vietnam. They drilled the point home constantly that our actions could mean life or death for ourselves and the other Marines in our unit. Strategy was often a topic of discussion – the strategy of finding and killing the enemy, the Viet Cong or NVA (North Vietnamese Army). On one hand it seemed like fun, sort of a game because the targets were fixed, easy to identify, and they didn't shoot back. In the back of my mind, I always knew that real combat would be much different. I knew that I'd have the security of other men backing me up. In return, as a radio operator, I would be helping to protect them. We'd be a team, and we'd have each other. We all knew that we could always count on each of the other Marines in our unit.

Our level of self-confidence increased now as we continued to advance our knowledge of weapons and our skills in using those weapons effectively. We were training in the art of combat for the sole purpose of fighting a war. Yet we did not know what war really was.

The time went by quickly as we reached the end of our combat infantry training. For the first time in over three months, we would finally be going home to our families before we reported to our MOS school. There we would learn the job the Marine Corps had chosen for us. I would become a Radio Telegraph Operator, but I didn't know what my combat duty in Vietnam would be like.

CHAPTER

# *THREE*

## RADIO TELEGRAPH SCHOOL

Radio Telegraph School was located at the Marine Corps Recruit Depot in San Diego, California. Like Parris Island, this was the west coast base where raw recruits were trained. I looked forward to the travel and seeing sights I had never seen before. So for now, the worst was over. The additional training that lay ahead would be completed in a classroom and not in the woods.

The trip home for a few weeks of rest and relaxation was well-deserved. We had earned our place among the ranks of the United States Marine Corps. As I put my dress uniform on, I felt proud to be a Marine. I was a new person – disciplined, well-trained, self-confident, motivated, ready to take on any challenge and ready to enter a world where I was sure I would receive respect and admiration for my service to my country. How naïve I was.

The day of graduation came without much fanfare. We departed the base individually, some taking cabs, some taking a bus to the airport or to the local bus station. As we left the base, we passed by the outdoor theater we had seen when we entered the base four weeks ago. We never did have the opportunity or time to relax and watch a movie. I felt a little bit of sadness as I left the men I had spent months with, trained with. I wasn't sure if I would ever see any of them again

In May, 1967, I reported for duty at the San Diego Marine Corps Recruit Depot. Sunny California was about as far away from my home in Norfolk, Virginia, as a kid my age could get. The California "babes" loved a Marine in uniform, as I quickly learned.

In 1967, a Marine in California seemed to be respected by the American people. I wore my dress uniform often and had free access to such attractions as the Balboa Zoo in San Diego, Disney Land in Anaheim, and Knott's Berry Farm in Buena Park. I met a girl from Whittier one weekend when a few of us went to Knott's Berry Farm. Her name was Kathy Williamson. I remember traveling to her house by bus often on weekends, and her parents treated me like one of the family. I had my own bedroom. Her mother would cook great meals for me, and they would let me use their car while I was there. The experience made me feel grown up, but I was only 19 and still didn't shave. Without the uniform, I just looked like another teenage boy.

Radio Telegraph School was 18 weeks long. The first 14 weeks would be spent learning Morse Code, sending and receiving meaningless messages to one another. We quickly settled into a routine. The life we were now living was much different from anything we had been through before.

We lived in a barracks again. We slept in a large squad bay with dozens of other Marines all enrolled in Radio Telegraph School. These were new men that I didn't know, not the men

I spent my first three months with. I made new friends and at least one new enemy.

California offered many sights and experiences for any young man with a little bit of money in his pocket. Downtown San Diego was a routine hangout for us. It had pool halls, theaters, tattoo parlors, bars, and even an old fashion burlesque show. Except for the bars, I spent time in them all.

The drinking age in California was 21. Most of us were too young to drink there; but if you were a Marine, you definitely drank, regardless of your age. The alternative for underage Marines was Tijuana, Mexico.

Maybe it was fortunate that I ended up getting my jaw broken in two places that night in Tijuana; I ran into a fist! We had just completed our 14 week course on Morse Code. With only 4 more weeks to go to final graduation, a group of us went to Tijuana to celebrate.

I was not much of a drinker. Frankly, I hated the taste of alcohol, especially beer. So I drank the hard stuff, flavored with other ingredients to help disguise the taste of the alcohol. We had been barhopping, and this was probably our fifth or sixth bar to try. By now, I was already feeling the effects of the drinks.

Some of our group was sitting at a table while I and a few others sat at the bar. I had just ordered a "Zombie." I have no idea what was in that drink, but it sure tasted good.

A fellow Marine in my class walked over to me and said "Hey, Hunt, I'll buy you a drink if you let me hit you." Had I been sober, I probably would have rejected the notion, but it sounded like a good deal to me at the time. I assumed he meant that he wanted to hit me in the muscle portion of my arm. So I tightened my left arm bringing my wrist around to my belly as you would if your arm was in a sling. As I held it tightly awaiting the impact, he hauled off and hit me with a tremendous force, square in my left jaw, knocking me out. I fell to the floor. When I regained consciousness, my mouth was bleeding, and I was in great pain. I ran to the bathroom to look in the mirror, and that is when I saw that the blow to my jaw had broken it.

The incident cost me a few teeth and three months in the Balboa Naval Hospital. It seems the guy who hit me had a grudge against me for some reason. After a few drinks at the bar, he decided to get his revenge. All I remember is picking myself up off the floor and feeling loose teeth. Two days later my mouth was wired shut and I was eating soupy mashed potatoes three times a day.

As it turned out, there was a silver lining to my misfortune. Every Marine who graduated from Radio Telegraph School received orders for Vietnam. Had I finished the last four weeks of school as scheduled, I would have been in Vietnam during the Tet Offensive. With all the fighting that took place then, I might have been killed. The guy who hit me might have been killed for that matter – I'll never know, I can't even remember his name.

The result of my medical setback was that after I was discharged from the hospital, the Marine Corps, in its wisdom, wanted me to repeat Radio Telegraph School. I challenged that logic by taking the final exam again and passing with flying colors.

Since there were no classes that I could pick up for my final four weeks of school, I was held back as Battalion "gopher" for 14 weeks. What that entailed was fetching coffee and donuts for the instructors every day, emptying trash cans, sweeping the floor and making runs to the PX to pick up cigarettes or whatever. It was what we called "bullshit duty!" But it was easy duty to say the least. I had weekends free and spent most of them with my girlfriend in Whittier.

In late February, 1968, I was able to pick up where I left off, the final four-week school on voice radio operations. Little did I know at the time that this part of my training was probably the most important of all.

I had spent 14 weeks learning Morse Code, sending and receiving messages by telegraph. This method of communication was antiquated. To this day, I do not know why a radio operator was required to know how to use Morse code. It was the voice radio that was actually used exclusively in Vietnam.

During that four-week school, I learned proper radio procedure. When communicating over a military radio, there was a discipline involved; and you spoke using a certain set of procedures. For example, when you had finished making a transmission, if you expected to receive a response from the person you were talking to, you would say the word "over." If you did not want a response, you would say the word "out." Unlike the war movies I had seen, you never said "over and out" together. It was not proper radio procedure. You said one or the other but not both at the same time.

The common radio used by the Marine Corps ground soldier was the PRC-25, pronounced "prick twenty-five." This radio was carried on the back. It weighed approximately 25 pounds and measured approximately 12 inches by 12 inches by 3 inches.

Two antennae were used with the radio, a regular antenna with a range of about 3 or 4 miles and a long range antenna with a range of about 18 miles.

We spent those four weeks talking on the radio to each other, sending messages the instructors gave us, and using the proper radio procedures they had taught us. They would listen to our transmissions using their own radio and would correct us if we said something incorrectly.

Most of the messages were in the form of requests for different types of supplies. We were not taught any specific jobs that existed for radio operators in Vietnam. I didn't learn about those jobs until I arrived there. This training gave the impression that all a radio operator did was send very routine messages requesting supplies and that it might even be a job performed in a secure area like a room in a large building. Nothing was taught about how the radio might actually be used in combat.

What started out as a 4-month tour in sunny California turned into a year, but graduation from radio school finally came. My new classmates and I waited 3 weeks for orders after graduation. When we finally did get them, all of us were ordered to Vietnam but only given 11 days leave time before having to report to Camp Pendleton for jungle training. Unfortunately, it was just enough time for a quick trip home and a few more days with my mother.

I was quickly reminded why I joined the Marine Corps, and it didn't take long before I was looking forward to returning to California and going to Vietnam. As always, every little thing I said or did was scrutinized and a subject for argument from her. Even after all the growing up I had done to become a Marine, I still could never win an argument with my mother; she was right and I was wrong, period. That's just the way she was.

Then it was back to California for the jungle training that was supposed to prepare me for Vietnam. Of course, that's what they told me in boot camp and that's what they told me in infantry training as well.

# CHAPTER

# *FOUR*

## JUNGLE TRAINING SCHOOL

After reporting to Camp Pendleton, California for Jungle Training School, I settled into another barracks. Some of my fellow classmates from Radio Telegraph School were there as well as many new men. The routine was the same – more "hurry up and wait," more medical exams and inoculations, more paperwork to fill out. I was issued a new weapon, the M-16 which looked and felt more like a Mattel toy than a real weapon. I had to learn how to break it down and put it back together in 30 seconds, blindfolded. I was taught how to keep it working, at least most of the time. The M-16 had quickly earned a reputation for being a sensitive weapon – sensitive to dirt, moisture, overuse. Ironically, these were the very conditions I would be subjected to routinely in Vietnam.

Like infantry training, my jungle training required me to fire my new weapon at different firing ranges. I went on patrols and learned that it's not easy to spot a target in the jungle just five feet away from you. This exercise began with a trail through the woods, terrain that supposedly was very similar to the terrain I would encounter in Vietnam. The mission was simple, walk the trail to the end and avoid the enemy. The enemy was a group of Marine instructors dressed up in black pajamas and Ho Chi Minh sandals, the typical dress of the Viet Cong.

There were two enemy forces in Vietnam – the Viet Cong and the North Vietnamese Army (NVA). The Viet Cong consisted of South Vietnamese men who sympathized with North Vietnam and fought for the North. They fought primarily in the mid and southern portions of South Vietnam, and they wore the black pajama dress. The NVA were trained, uniformed soldiers from North Vietnam; and they fought primarily in the northern portion of South Vietnam where it was easy to infiltrate across the DMZ (Demilitarized Zone or the border between North and South Vietnam).

Not quite knowing what to expect or even what to look for, our patrol walked for a few hundred yards, slowly, cautiously, eyes scanning the foliage and terrain around us. We were all a bit tense with anticipation; it just looked like the woods back home, trees, brush, dirt, nothing more, nothing less.

Crack, crack, crack…. Automatic weapons fire erupted all around us, close, very close by. Instinctively we hit the dirt which just made matters worse, being low to the ground like that made it even more difficult to see what was going on and where the shooting was coming from. It seemed to be coming from all around us, in front, in back, on both sides of the trail. Like the men who were shooting at us, we had blanks in our M-16's; and we just started shooting, pointing the weapons outward from the trail. It was a panic stricken moment, and I could feel the surge of adrenaline pass through my body. I knew it wasn't real, but it sure felt real.

As quickly as the shooting started, it ended and we lay on the ground in silence, not quite knowing what to do next. An instructor stepped forward and told us to get up. As we rose, the enemy actors emerged from the brush all around us. Some were so close you could almost touch them. We never saw a single one of them when they sprang their ambush on us. To make matters worse, the instructor told us that had this been a real ambush in Vietnam, we all would have been killed in a matter of seconds. That was a sobering thought.

The men who ambushed us carried real enemy weapons, the Russian AK-47 and the Chinese SKS. These weapons had a very distinct sound when fired at you, even when they carried blanks. The M-16 on the other hand, sounded completely different. That was one of the points the instructor wanted to make to us. Learn to recognize the sound of an enemy weapon.

The most interesting part of my jungle training was about booby traps. There was the pungi pit, a hole in the ground with sharpened bamboo spikes sticking up that would penetrate your body like a sharp knife. In Vietnam, the tips of these spikes would be covered with poison.

There were other similar spiked traps that would fall from trees or spring out at you unexpectedly. C-ration cans also made good booby traps. An American hand grenade with the pin pulled would fit neatly inside one of these cans just holding the spoon in place. A wire would be attached to the grenade and strung across a trail. Trip the wire and the grenade would come out of the can releasing the spoon and arming the grenade.

My favorite one was the neat booby trap that utilized a spent M-72 LAAW (light armor anti-tank weapon), a modern day version of a disposable bazooka. This weapon fired a 66 millimeter projectile which could penetrate the armor on a tank. Once it had been fired, it could not be reloaded. The weapon was disposable and only contained one round. It was light weight, and often several could be carried by one soldier. It had a shoulder strap so that it could be slung across the shoulder or across the back with the strap slung across the chest.

Six hand grenades could be neatly stuffed inside the spent LAAW, with the pins pulled. A wire attached to the trap door end cover would trip the booby trap. When hung in a tree, a radio operator's antenna would trigger the trap by hitting the wire which would open the trap door dropping those six LIVE grenades on his head. Wow, I really needed to know that! Maybe, staying home and putting up with my mother wasn't such a bad idea after all.

Another fun part of jungle training was the day we spent in a prisoner of war camp, simulated of course. We were given one bowl of rice and a carrot to eat all day; and when it got dark, we had to escape and make our way back to a safe camp area three miles away with nothing but the stars to navigate by. All we were told was what direction, south I think, the safe camp was from the POW camp. To make things a little more difficult, men were waiting in all directions around the camp, hidden in brush and trees, to recapture us and scare the hell out of us to boot. How I ever managed to get through jungle training still amazes me even today. But I survived, I graduated, and I was officially qualified to fight in Vietnam.

We spent another week getting shots and filling out endless forms and paperwork. We were briefed on the Code of Conduct, a set of rules to follow if you were taken prisoner, before we finally packed our sea bags and got on a bus for Travis Air Force Base in California. There, we boarded civilian aircraft and departed the United States around midnight.

So as one journey ended, from civilian to combat ready Marine, a new journey began. It was April, 1968. I had joined the Marines in December, 1966; and after 16 months of training, minus a few months spent in the hospital, the adventure of my life had now begun. I was finally on my way to Vietnam for a 13-month tour of duty for which I was well-trained *but very ill-prepared.*

*LAAW – Courtesy of Wikipedia.org*

# CHAPTER

# *FIVE*

## WELCOME TO THE NAM

It was April 28, 1968. After a long flight from Okinawa, the Philippines, I landed in Da Nang, Vietnam. It was hot and dry, over 100 degrees. I went through some simple processing at the terminal and picked up my seabag. I was loaded on a large, open truck. A 5-minute drive took me to the main processing center.

I carried my seabag, orders, and personnel records with me. I wore my fatigues and boots. I stood out like a sore thumb. Everyone I saw was wearing the standard jungle fatigues and jungle boots. The uniforms looked faded, old, and dirty. Compared to them, I looked like a shiny new penny.

The barracks were simple structures made mostly of plywood with windows that had no glass, only window screening. There was no air conditioning. Men slept on cots. There were rows and rows of these buildings all lined up in typical military fashion. This might not be bad duty; I could live here for a year.

Again we played the traditional Marine Corps game, "Hurry up and wait." After several hours of waiting, filling out some forms, and waiting some more, I was finally given a new set of orders. I was to report to 1$^{st}$ Battalion, 3$^{rd}$ Marine Regiment, 3$^{rd}$ Marine Division in Quang Tri, wherever that was. I later learned that Vietnam was broken down into sectors and I was going to "I Corps" (pronounced eye core). I Corps was the area closest to North Vietnam, along the DMZ (demilitarized zone). I would learn the significance of that soon enough.

Several of us were put back on trucks with our seabags, and taken back to the airport terminal we came through when we landed. We checked in and gave up one copy of our orders and were told to wait in the terminal. They would call us when our plane was ready.

Looking out from the terminal, I saw what appeared to be a very large city, but there were no sky-scrapers. It looked nothing like I had expected. Of course, the air base was all around me, lots of airplanes, combat aircraft, and fighter jets. I didn't know much about combat aircraft, so I didn't recognize what type of planes they were. That would soon change.

I could see other buildings in the distance, small buildings but none of the straw huts I had expected to see. Lots of vehicular traffic moved quickly around the terminal area and in the distance. It hardly seemed like a war zone here. Maybe my tour of duty in Vietnam wouldn't be so bad after all.

Quang Tri, I wondered what that was like, probably similar to this place. It had to be big. I was going by plane, so it must have an airport. Yep, this might not be too bad, except for the heat.

I was finally called to load up and board my plane for Quang Tri. I hoped to get a window seat so I could look out at the land below as we flew to Quang Tri.

Walking out onto the tarmac, I looked around for the jet airliner expecting to board a civilian aircraft like the one I flew in on. Instead, all I saw was some sort of propeller driven military aircraft, which I later learned was a C-130 cargo plane. We boarded the plane from the rear, walking up a ramp that opens from the back of the plane.

There were no seats, no chairs of any kind. We simply sat down on the metal floor in rows in a very uncomfortable position. There must have been 100 men in the plane when we took off. Of course, in that position, you could not see out the few tiny windows in the side of the aircraft. The noise from the propeller driven engines, 4 of them, was almost deafening.

Our flight ended in about 30 minutes, and not a minute too soon. I was getting cramped and uncomfortable. The plane came to a stop on the makeshift runway which was made of a metal grating. The ramp was lowered, and we anxiously stood and exited the aircraft. As we were herded off, we were directed to a makeshift terminal made of plywood, similar to the huts I saw in Da Nang. Sand bag bunkers were all around. I had not seen or learned anything about bunkers in all my prior training.

Many of the men were new like I was. We showed a sergeant our orders and were given instructions as to where to go to get to our unit. I was told to go outside to the road and hitchhike south to Quang Tri. We had not landed in Quang Tri. We were in Dong Ha. The "rear" of my unit was in Quang Tri. Rear of the unit, what did that mean?

I grabbed my seabag and headed outside. So far, this was nothing like I had expected. The road was nothing more than a dirt road running north/south, Rt. 1, I believe. Looking east, I could see gray smoke and red dust rising above the trees. Artillery shells were impacting several miles away, and I could hear the explosions moments after seeing the impact. I didn't know this was artillery impacting. I had to ask someone what it was that I was seeing.

There were several "veterans" standing around waiting. They looked old for young kids, dirty, tired, battle worn. Their uniforms looked like they'd been worn forever, faded and grungy. Their boots lacked any kind of polish or shine. They were called jungle boots, part leather, part canvas. The leather was a dull grey, and the canvas was faded and dirty. The vets looked like they had walked a thousand miles in those boots.

I talked to one of the vets and learned that the explosions we were seeing to the east were related to an attack by the NVA (North Vietnamese Army) on the Cua Viet River. The river was a major supply route for materials and supplies to the U.S. military units operating in the I Corps area. Supply boats would bring in supplies from larger transport ships out in the Gulf of Tonkin coming inland on the river to Dong Ha. The NVA were trying to take control of the river and perhaps even Dong Ha. This fight had just broken out in the past few days, and some Marine units were heavily involved in the fight.

Still thinking about the artillery fire I saw off in the distance, I reviewed the months and months of training I had been through that was supposed to have prepared me for this combat duty. I had fired all kinds of weapons, been on all kinds of maneuvers and patrols; but in all that training, no one had ever talked to us about artillery or any kind of large, crew-served, enemy weapons.

The term "crew-served" meant that the weapon took more than one man to fire it. This included artillery, rockets and mortars as well as some smaller weapons. As I reflected on the subject, it dawned on me that I really had no idea what kind of damage these weapons could cause. The explosions to the east looked to be fairly large since they were clearly visible at such a long distance, several miles. "Geez, I'd hate to be close to something like that exploding. Do the North Vietnamese have such weapons?" I wondered. No, they couldn't have them here in South Vietnam, and surely those weapons couldn't fire from North Vietnam and hit us. I was beginning to wonder what else I would encounter that I had not been prepared for.

Standing there on a dirt road in South Vietnam awaiting a ride south to my unit just didn't seem quite real. No one was shooting at me; and yet there, in the distance, someone was shooting at someone else and fighting was evidently going on. It wasn't anything like I had imagined. I'd seen the World War II movies with John Wayne, but this was a different kind of war than any of the movie's I had seen.

"Can you tell me how to get to 1st Battalion, 3rd Marine Regiment in Quang Tri?" I asked one of the vets.

"Yeah man. Ya' wait for a truck or something to come along, and ya' catch yourself a ride south. Tell the dude to let ya' off at Quang Tri base. That's where 1/3 is, man."

"Okay, thanks, man." I said.

So I waited – hurry up and wait. A convoy of big trucks and jeeps came by soon enough, and I stuck out my thumb in the typical hitchhiking style. A truck stopped.

"Where ya' headed, man?" the driver asked.

"Quang Tri Base?" I replied.

"Hop on."

So I tossed my seabag onto the back of the truck and climbed aboard. The ride was peaceful enough. We passed some South Vietnamese civilians wearing the traditional black pajamas, sandals, and those funny straw hats that looked like large, wide cones. This was the common attire of the Vietnamese peasants and farmers. It was also the common uniform of the Viet Cong soldier.

I often saw civilians carrying things, usually bundles hanging from each end of a large stick. They'd balance the stick on their shoulders with one arm wrapped around the forward portion. They walked quickly as if in a hurry and paid no attention to the convoy of trucks passing them.

I wondered what was in the bundles. Explosives? I recalled my jungle training and some of the lectures. The Viet Cong would look like any other Vietnamese civilian during the day and often attack the American units at night. I wondered if some of these civilians were Viet Cong? I hoped not, I hadn't been issued a weapon yet.

We passed small villages that were homes of a simple society. This was more like I had expected – straw huts, no running water, no electricity, a subsistence kind of life. It was as though I had passed through a time warp.

To each side of the road were the well-known rice paddies. I saw civilians hunched over in the knee deep muddy water, working the rice fields. Straw huts, rice paddies, hard work, and nothing modern like I was accustomed to.

I had to wonder just why these people needed defending. Could communism possibly impact these people in any manner that would pose a threat to the United States? Already I was beginning to search for reasons to be here, justification for the war. It wasn't making much sense to me, so far. Today, as I look back, it appears to me that the only thing that threatened the lives of these people was civilization itself. No form of government would change their lives. These were simple, almost primitive people. Their way of life certainly posed no threat to the American people. I have to wonder how communism in Vietnam would have posed a threat to our modern and powerful nation. I think it was the mentality of our nation at that time – stop Communism at all cost.

The ride took about 30 minutes or so, and the terrain had changed, becoming more open and sandy. I could see a military base on the right as we slowed to a stop.

"Quang Tri, man," the driver shouted out to me.

After tossing my seabag off, I climbed down from the truck. Rows of large tents stood in front of me a few hundred yards away. Men were moving about in meaningless activity. It was quiet, peaceful. No war here, I thought.

I picked up my seabag, threw it over my shoulder and headed for the row of tents. As I approached, I stopped to ask someone where I was to go.

"Corporal, can you tell me where I need to go?" I asked as I handed the man my orders.

He glanced at them briefly and said, "Yeah man, H & S Company. Follow that row of tents, you'll see a sign." He pointed in the general direction.

So I headed off in that direction. It was difficult walking in the hot sand with my seabag on my shoulder. I wondered what they would do with my seabag. Would I have to carry all of this stuff everywhere I went? No, they wouldn't make you do that, would they?

I saw the tent with a sign that indicated "H & S Company, 1st Bn. 3rd Marines." I entered and dropped my seabag by my side as I handed my personnel records and orders to a man sitting at a makeshift desk.

"Lance Corporal Hunt, welcome to 1/3, man. I'll get ya' checked in; then you need to go to supply and pick up your equipment. You'll leave your bag there. It'll get stored until your tour of duty is up. You'll be assigned to H & S company for now. Any questions?"

"Yes sir, where is the supply tent?" I asked.

"Come on man, ya' know the drill, I ain't no officer, I work for a living. Go out the door, turn right, third tent on your right."

The clerk kept my records, stamped my orders, tore off a copy and handed it to me. I hoisted the seabag over my shoulder and headed out the door. A moment later I entered the supply tent and dropped my bag again, handing another Marine the copy of my orders.

He looked at my orders for a moment. "Private Hunt, 2533 huh? Great, we just had a radio operator killed yesterday, they'll be glad to see you!"

Wow, there it is! The reality of the war struck me like a brick up the side of my head. I was a 2533, radio and telegraph operator. That was my MOS, military occupation specialty. Another radio operator, like me, had just been killed; I was going to replace him.

I was issued my combat gear – jungle fatigues, jungle boots, OD green (olive drab) t-shirt and skivvies, a jungle hat, helmet, 4 canteens, web belt, medical bandage, gas mask, an M-16 with 2 bandoliers of ammunition and 3 hand grenades. I was told to change uniforms and store my standard fatigues and boots in my seabag. The Marine put my name and service number on a tag and tied it to the handle of the seabag. I would leave the bag there where it would be stored until I left country in 13 months.

"Go down this row of tents and find an empty rack in one of them. You'll be going to the field tomorrow morning. Ya' hungry, man? Mess tent's two rows over. Get ya' something to eat."

I headed for a tent and rack first. I just wanted to find my new sleeping quarters first and get settled. Food could wait. I found a tent with about a dozen other marines in it, and I was relieved to find out that I wasn't the only "FNG" (fucking new guy) here. There were several other "cherries" who had recently arrived and were waiting to go to the field.

I dropped my gear at an empty rack, introduced myself (as if somebody really cared), and tried to find out what was going on.

Our unit was engaged in a firefight in the village of Dai Do along Song Bo Dieu River, a branch of the Cua Viet River. One company had been overrun, and other units were involved in the fight. The NVA wanted to take control of the river which was a vital supply route for U.S. supplies into the country. With control of the river, the NVA could then move in and take over Dong Ha and eventually move on Quang Tri, the provincial capital of that region. Dong Ha was the headquarters for the entire Third Marine Division.

From what I was told, this was a major battle; we were up against the 320th NVA Division. I was told that we were greatly outnumbered, and I was still thinking about the radio operator who had been killed – the one I was going to replace. I recalled the stories I had heard in radio school. The life expectancy of a radio operator in a firefight was 15 seconds. That big antenna sticking high in the air was a dead giveaway, like a big arrow pointing downward saying "Here I am, shoot me!" Needless to say, my apprehension of what was to come prevented me from getting much sleep that night, not to mention the fact that sleeping on a cot with no cushioning was not the most comfortable way to sleep. Also, the heat was something I was definitely going to have to get used to. California was hot, but Viet Nam was damn hot!

The next day, April 29th, three of us were told to go back out to that dirt road and hitchhike to the bridge over the Song Do Dieu River where Route 9 intersects Route 1. There would be a dock on the right just past the airfield I had landed at the day before. We would be catching a boat from there and would be taken to 1/3 headquarters in the field – a village called Thon Lap Thach on the south side of the river. We were to take everything we were issued, and we wouldn't be coming back to the rear area for a good while.

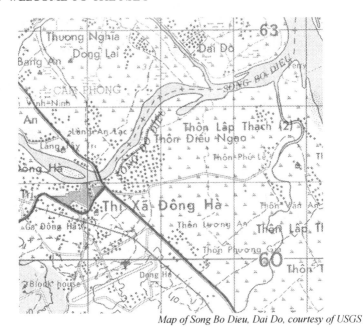

*Map of Song Bo Dieu, Dai Do, courtesy of USGS*

The other two men were grunts, typical fighting Marines, 0300's, which was their MOS. We had no idea of what we were soon to experience. I was surprised that no other experienced Marine was with us to tell us what to do and when to do it. We were totally on our own, expected to travel in hostile territory "out to the field" and locate our unit in no man's land.

The equipment we carried was heavy. The flak jacket was a sleeveless jacket lined with a kind of fiberglass plating that would protect you against shrapnel fragments to a limited extent. It was not bullet proof and it weighed ten pounds. The helmet was steel and weighed six pounds by itself. A pack was carried on your back that contained your food (C-rations), some socks, a poncho and a poncho liner (used as a blanket or a pillow), and any personal items you wished to carry such as writing paper, envelopes, pen and toiletries.

You wore a special ammo belt around your waist. Attached to the belt were 4 canteens of water, several ammo pouches with 2 or 3 magazines of ammo, 18 rounds per magazine, your bayonet, and your gas mask.

The ammo belt was held up by straps that went over your shoulder. A medical bandage in a small pouch was attached to one of the straps. Typically, hand grenades were also attached by the pins to the straps which had cloth strings dangling from them to tie the grenades to. When you needed to throw the grenade, you would simply pull on it. The pin, being attached to the shoulder strap, would come out arming the grenade automatically, and you'd throw it. We also carried our M-16 and two bandoliers of ammunition, 300 rounds in each. I had 3 hand grenades on my shoulder straps. I also carried 3 smoke grenades that one of the grunts had given me. These hung in a similar fashion from my back pack. All of this equipment made movement difficult in the 100 degree heat. But it was all a necessity and you didn't want to be without any of it.

It didn't take long before we caught a ride and had arrived at the dock. The dock wasn't really a dock like you might have seen on a lake or at the beach. It was actually a large barren area next to the river with a reinforced wall so boats could pull next to it and unload their cargo.

There was a large sandbagged bunker in the center area of the dock; and, in one corner, was a tall tower with sandbags around the top portion. The tower had a tin roof and enabled men to view the surrounding area in all directions.

A few men were in the bunker playing cards; others were in the tower, peering out occasionally with binoculars. A tracked vehicle called an "otter" was off to one side, and a small Navy boat was tied to the dock. Men loitered on the boat.

We told one of the men that we were supposed to catch a boat to 1/3's headquarters and asked him what he wanted us to do. He told us to drop our gear and wait for further instructions.

"Typical Marine Corps," I thought, "Hurry up and wait."

The river went east to west from the Gulf of Tonkin. Typically, Navy river craft would travel up and down the river taking men and supplies to and from points along the way. We were supposed to travel out to our unit on one of these craft, when and if it ever arrived. We were informed that the river was temporarily closed due to the fighting in a village to the northeast.

Minutes turned to hours. Soon the day was nearing an end. The river craft that was to take us out to the unit never came. However, the day was not one without some events to remember.

The first incident took place a few hours after we had arrived. We began taking sniper fire from some small arms (AK47's most likely), and we scrambled to take cover in the bunker. The fire came from a tree line on the opposite shore of the river.

Three shots were fired in quick succession at some of the men loitering around the dock. It happened quickly and without warning; then it was over. A few of the more seasoned vets laughed it off and made some comment about "Charlie" being a poor shot.

In mid afternoon, I heard a swishing sound and seconds later an explosion. An enemy mortar slammed into the track vehicle parked only 50 meters away. Again, we were scampering for cover. I dove for the ground and covered my head with my hands, as if that would protect me. It was becoming clear to me that I should stay closer to that sandbagged bunker which provided much better protection than the hand over my head!

Incoming mortars were not something I had been trained for. I was petrified as the mortars began dropping all around us, one every 30 seconds or so.

I guess the first thought that ran through my mind was death. Was I going to get killed before I even made it out to my unit? I felt all alone. Even though I had come here with two other men, I didn't know them. We had only spent a short time together and were all inexperienced in actual combat situations.

The next thought that went through my mind was attack. Were we going to be attacked by ground forces? What direction would they come from? How many might attack us? What do we do? Who's in command?

I had lots of questions and no answers. The mortar attack lasted just a few minutes, but it brought the reality of war home to me quickly. I had survived my first encounter with real enemy fire. First it was a sniper, then a mortar attack. This was just my first day in Vietnam. How was I ever going to survive 13 months of this?

I quickly realized that all of that training I had been subjected to did not prepare me for what I had just experienced. Most of my training pertained to the use of many weapons of the Marine Corps. None of my training included how to defend against attacks from enemy mortars. My training was offensive in nature, not defensive. What other weapons did the enemy have that I hadn't been trained to defend against?

As the day drew to an end, it was clear that we weren't going out to the field. We talked among ourselves and decided that we should report back to the battalion headquarters in Quang Tri. We walked back up the road to the highway where we once again caught a ride from a passing vehicle.

When we arrived back at the headquarters compound, no one seemed surprised that we didn't get out to the field that day; it was as though everyone knew what was going on but us. The company gunnery sergeant (gunny) told us to try again first thing tomorrow morning.

I dropped my gear by the bunk I had slept on the night before and headed for the mess hall. Those C-rations I had eaten earlier in the day just didn't do much to fill me up.

On April 30th, the day started much the same as the day before. Having learned a lesson, we stayed close to the bunker, in case we received incoming mortars or sniper fire again. But that day turned out to be peaceful. Another lesson learned was that each day in the Nam is different, and every day is unpredictable.

By late afternoon, we had concluded that we weren't going to the field that day either. I heard a lot of small arms fire and explosions to the east; probably from artillery or air-strikes I was told. I could tell that a fierce battle was being waged not far from here. Again, I worried if we would come under attack also. "What was it like to be in an actual battle?" I wondered.

Shortly after we arrived back at battalion, the gunny told us to get our gear; a boat was waiting for us at the dock. We were definitely going out to the field this evening. "It figures, typical Marine Corps, a three-ring circus and the word changes constantly," I muttered to myself.

A company jeep carried the three of us back down to the dock for the second time that day. I wondered why they couldn't have taken us to the dock the previous times in this jeep, rather than make us hitchhike on our own.

When we arrived at the dock, I was expecting to see a Navy landing craft like the ones I had seen in the John Wayne movies landing on the beaches of Normandy or someplace like that. I was surprised to see that a ten-foot "john boat" was waiting for us. It had a small gas motor mounted on the back. "At least they weren't expecting us to row the thing out to the field," I thought.

A seasoned vet was waiting for us in the boat. His clothes looked old, as if he had worn them for a hundred years. They were caked with red dust and the knees of the trousers were blackened. He wore a camouflage jungle hat, and his long hair stuck out from under it. Long hair was a sight you don't see often in the military, especially on a Marine.

"Listen up! Unstrap your helmets and lock and load your weapon. If the boat capsizes, get rid of your helmet immediately; the weight of the damn thing will drown you. But hang on to your weapon, you just might need it. Swim to the southern shore because Charlie is on the north shore. Any questions?"

"Yeah, which is the southern shore?" I asked.

"It's on your right as we head down river. Mount up!"

The helmet will drown me, swim to the southern shore, Charlie's on the north shore (and who is Charlie anyway?). This doesn't sound good. The apprehension was quickly building up inside of me.

I unstrapped my helmet and put a fully loaded magazine into my new M-16. It seemed strange to chamber a round and click the safety off. The only time I had ever done that before was on a supervised firing range.

The trip down the river lasted about 10 or 15 minutes. We zigzagged from shore to shore, the small motor racing at full speed. I crouched low in the boat trying to be a less conspicuous target. I felt like a mouse being sent into a cage full of lions. This was where the war was. This was where the fighting was that we had heard earlier in the day. Not knowing what to expect, I expected the worst would happen at any moment.

The boat began to slow down as it approached the southern shoal. I could see a village through the woods ahead. There were some bamboo hooches (straw huts) and a small stone building, which I later learned was called a "pagoda" or temple of worship.

As the boat slowed, several men ran out to help us. Suddenly there was mass confusion, as noises unfamiliar to me filled the air. Bullets were flying by my head and I heard the distinct cracking sound of a Russian AK-47 assault rifle. It sounded just like the one I had heard in jungle training on that patrol where everyone got "killed." The bullets made a whizzing sound all around me, repeatedly, rhythmically.

A man on the shore reached out his arm, motioning me to take hold of his hand so he could pull me out of the boat. As I moved to grab his hand, it disappeared as though he had yanked it away. As I saw him jerk backwards, I realized that he had been hit. It was as though he had been pulled back by a rope tied around his waist.

The adrenaline raced through my body now as I sprang from the boat and ran towards the village. I continued to hear the crack of the AK-47's, and dirt was being kicked up around me as the bullets struck the ground. I had become the target now.

The pagoda was 20 meters or so in front of me, and the land sloped upward making it more difficult to run with all the equipment I was carrying.

"Corpsman up, corpsman up!" a Marine shouted.

I had reached the pagoda and dropped to the ground behind it. The others followed me, and two other men dragged the Marine who had been hit trying to help me. He was unconscious, but wasn't bleeding.

*A Typical Pagoda*

The corpsman ran to the injured man's side and dropped his medical bag on the ground. I sat frozen as I watched the "doc" do his job.

The corpsman wasn't any older than I, but he worked with the confidence of a skilled doctor. It was clear that he had been in this situation many times.

The injured man was lucky. The bullet had only grazed his helmet, not penetrated it. The steel pot had saved his life and I was relieved to know that some of this heavy equipment really did work; it really did protect you. I was also thankful to know that the man was going to be okay; after all, he was trying to help *me* when he was hit by that bullet. The man had suffered a concussion and needed to be medivaced to a rear area aid station.

"One four man up!" the corpsman shouted.

Another Marine ran to the injured man's side, a radio operator.

"I need a routine medivac, I've gotta get this man to an aid station."

"Candy Tuff one four, this is Bravo one four, over."

"Bravo, Candy Tuff, over."

"Roger, I need a routine medivac, over."

"Roger, routine medivac, out."

Now that was more like the teamwork I had been taught in infantry training. Both men clearly knew what they were doing. I saw no officers or non-com's telling them what to do. They knew what to do; and they did their jobs as a team, working together to handle the situation. I was impressed.

A few minutes later a mechanized vehicle, an otter, arrived. The otter was a tracked vehicle used to carry troops inside. It was about the size of a typical automobile and carried a 50 caliber machine gun on top. A hatch provided access to the gun. The otter was to carry us to the battalion field headquarters. The back gate came down, and we climbed inside the cramped quarters. The gate closed and we headed off through the woods on a small dirt road.

The ride lasted another 10 or 15 minutes. The dust that was kicked up by the tracks of the vehicle was thick as smoke. When we finally arrived at headquarters, we looked as though we had been in the field for months. We were covered with red dust from head to toe. As I stepped out of the vehicle, my foot sank ankle deep in red dust. It looked like solid ground, and I was startled when I discovered that it wasn't. I lost my balance and almost fell.

I reported for duty and was sent to the Battalion communications (commo) section. The commo section consisted of several radio operators and a few officers. One, a captain, was the Air Liaison Officer. He told me that I would become a part of the Tactical Air Control Party (TAC Party). A sergeant named Ralph Gordon would train me to be a "one four man."

*Ralph Gordon*

One four man. I had heard that term earlier that day. That was what the doc had called that radio operator. The one four man had radioed for a medivac chopper to get the injured marine flown out to an aid station. So that's what I would be doing during my tour of duty in the Nam.

I spent the rest of the day talking with Gordon and the other radio operators in the TAC Party. There was much I had to learn. I knew how to operate the radio. What I didn't know was how to do the job of a tactical air controlman.

Gordon spent time explaining the different functions of the one four man and how each function related to the operations of the unit.

Tactical air control was a vital support function in the Marine line company. It was the one four man who brought in the medivac and resupply choppers (helicopters). It was the one four man who controlled the air-strikes with the aid of an aerial observer (AO). It was the one four man who was responsible for telling the AO where the lead friendly elements were and where the enemy was. This required him to be close to those elements and to have radio communications with them.

The one four man had to know the different types of ordinance used by the fixed-wing aircraft that flew support, as well as the ordinance carried by the UH-1 or Huey helicopters and gunships. The one four man had to know the bursting radius of these ordinances so that he could decide which ordinance would be best suited for the particular combat situation. The ordinance dropped had to be effective on the enemy target but also could not cause harm to nearby friendly troops.

Everything Gordon explained to me was new. None of it was taught to me in all of that training I had received back in the "world." This was on the job training (OJT) in every respect, and I needed to learn it quickly. It was a lot of information to absorb.

The fixed-wing aircraft I would most likely have to call on for support would be the A-4 Skyhawk, the F-4 Phantom, or the A-6 Intruder. Each had certain weapons capabilities, and the aircraft that would be sent to provide support depended on the ordinance requirements specified by the one four man.

The fixed-wing aircraft were capable of carrying a wide variety of ordinances. Their heavy ordinance consisted of 250 pound, 500 pound, 1000 pound, and 2000 pound bombs.

There were "snake" bombs, 250 pound and 500 pound bombs with fins that would deploy when dropped. The fins would slow the bomb down which enabled the aircraft to escape the blast of the exploding bomb. These bombs were dropped from a lower altitude making them more accurate. They also made a distinct swishing sound as they came down, and they wiggled in a manner similar to a snake.

The most deadly ordinance carried by the fixed-wing aircraft was the 500 pound canister of napalm. Napalm was like a thick glue that, when exploded, created an intense fireball and stuck to anything and everything. The exploding napalm would suck the air right out of your lungs. If you weren't killed by the fireball, you would die from suffocation if you were close enough to it.

The bursting radius of the other bombs was based on their weight. For example, a 500 pound bomb had a bursting radius of 500 meters. That meant that if you were within 500 meters of the exploding bomb, there was a very high probability that you would be killed or wounded from the shrapnel of the bomb. The larger the bomb, the wider the bursting radius; thus, the farther friendly troops had to be from the exploding bomb.

These bombs were not dropped one at a time either. They were dropped in pairs or multiples. These weapons were designed to inflict maximum casualties on the enemy. I had to wonder if the enemy had such weapons he could use against us. Gordon told me they had some Russian fixed-wing aircraft but none had ever flown close ground support for NVA troops operating in South Vietnam. I was relieved to know that.

In addition to fixed-wing aircraft there were attack helicopters such as the UH-1 Huey Gunship and AH-1 Huey Cobra. These helicopters usually carried 60 millimeter rockets. The UH-1 carried up to six M-60 machine guns, which fired a 7.62 millimeter bullet. The Cobra's carried Gatling guns which fired 20 millimeter bullets in very rapid succession. The Cobra also carried a rapid fire grenade launcher, which fired a 40 millimeter explosive round. These helicopters usually flew in pairs and provided an awesome amount of firepower for close air support where the enemy was very close to friendly troops.

I also learned that under special circumstances, the one four man might need to order air support from Spooky or Puff the Magic Dragon. Both are propeller-driven aircraft that have either a 20 millimeter Gatling gun (Spooky) installed in the waist of the plane or a 105 millimeter Howitzer (Puff). The gun fires out and down from the waist of the plane. A crew inside operates the weapon. Both aircraft drop flares that light up the target, and they are generally flown at night time.

In addition to the various aircraft that provide weapon support, it is the job of the one four man to bring resupply choppers into the unit landing zone. These may be CH-46 helicopters, CH-53 helicopters, or UH-1 helicopters. The CH-46 has a double rotor and is often used to carry up to 18 combat equipped troops. More commonly, it carries resupplies inside a net that hangs from a hook on the bottom of the aircraft. When the net full of supplies is placed on the ground, it is released by the pilot.

The CH-53 is a larger helicopter which can carry troops internally or supplies inside a net in the same manner as the CH-46. The smaller UH-1, Huey, can carry approximately six combat equipped soldiers, and it also has a hook for carrying nets of supplies.

Although the one four man was commonly an enlisted man, sergeant or lower in rank, he carried a lot of responsibility. Without the one four man, a combat company would have a difficult time maneuvering effectively against the enemy. The one four man brought awesome firepower to the aid of the company as well as a quick response to medical and logistical needs. This was a great deal of responsibility for a young Marine. I felt proud that I would have such an important job.

The one four man carried a sidearm, usually a 45-caliber pistol, but his real weapon was his radio. The common radio used by the one four man and other radio operators in the unit was the PRC-25, the same radio I had been trained to use in radio school.

This radio could transmit and receive up to approximately 21 miles and used different antennae for such communications. The standard antenna was a 3 foot "tape" antenna. The name came from the way the antenna was made, similar to a carpenter's measuring tape. It had a range of approximately 2.5 miles.

When more range was needed, the radio operator installed the whip antenna. This was a 7 section folding metal antenna that was approximately 15 feet long. Most radio operators hated to use this antenna because it made the operator more vulnerable to attack by a sniper. The tall antenna gave his position away even when the operator himself might not be easily visible due to the jungle foliage.

The radio was powered by a dry cell battery which added another 2 pounds to the radio operator's load. Since the battery would only last about 20 hours, several spare batteries had to be carried; and a resupply of batteries was constantly needed.

Gordon assured me that he would remain with me in the days to come, until he felt that I knew enough about the job of the one four man to take over on my own. My OJT had just begun, and I would learn much in the days ahead from actual combat. For now I was content taking things slowly.

The village we were in was on a branch of the Cua Viet River. To the north of the river, in a village called Dai Do, 2/4 ($2^{nd}$ Battalion $4^{th}$ Marine Regiment) had been in heavy contact with a sizeable NVA force. That was the fighting I had heard when we were at the dock waiting for a boat to take us to the field.

The enemy was trying to take control of the river and was staging an attack on Dong Ha. It was imperative that we not let the NVA succeed, or the entire I Corps area of responsibility could be in jeopardy. If Dong Ha fell to the enemy, the provincial capital of Quang Tri would be next.

That night, I stood radio watch at the Battalion headquarters. I was instructed to write down everything that came across several radios. These radios were set up to monitor the company radio traffic from 2/4.

A spooky was on station that night dropping flares over the village and strafing it with its 20 millimeter cannons. I could hear the pilot talking to the one four man and it became clearer why they called it "spooky." There was a lot of vibration from the plane's propeller driven engines which made the pilot's voice vibrate and sound sort of spooky.

Since I was new in country, the radio traffic made little sense to me. I struggled to keep up with it at times, trying to write down every word I heard. In radio telegraph school, I had learned that the average person can only write approximately 12 words per minute. Because the Morse Code we had to take came much faster, we had been required to learn how to type at least 30 words per minute. I sure could have used a typewriter that night, which would have made it much easier to keep up with the rapid transmissions that often came across the radios.

I monitored transmissions about probing of the company's lines, listening posts seeing figures in the dark, and an ambush springing its trap on an unsuspecting enemy squad. I was thankful that it wasn't me at the other end of those radios. I just wasn't prepared for that sort of thing yet. I had been in country less than a week, and it was still all too confusing to me.

I briefed the new radio operator as he came to relieve me in the early morning hours. I felt it was important that he fully understood the situation; it seemed pretty serious to me anyway.

He shrugged his shoulders and said "Yeah man, so what else is new? Welcome to the Nam!"

*A Typical Vietnamese Village*

# CHAPTER

# *SIX*

## THE BATTLE OF DAI DO

On May 4, 1968, we were told to pack up our gear and prepare to move out. We were going into the village of Dai Do to relieve 2/4. Within an hour, amtraks arrived to take us across the Song Bo Dieu River. These were tracked vehicles similar to a tank but without a gun. Although they could carry personnel inside, we would ride outside, on top of the vehicle. After climbing aboard and waiting a few minutes for everyone to get situated, the vehicle moved forward. Fifteen minutes later, the vehicle began to cross the river.

There were several vehicles ahead of ours which had already stopped on the northern bank of the river. The Marines dismounted those vehicles and began to move north in a single file. They proceeded cautiously towards Dai Do.

*Amtrak Vehicle*

The vehicle I was on came to a stop in the middle of the river for about 30 minutes while the lead elements ahead of us moved into the village. That feeling of fear started to settle inside of me once again as I began thinking about what might happen if we suddenly came under enemy fire.

I didn't know how deep the river was, but surely it was over my head. With all of the equipment I was carrying, I knew that I would quickly sink to the bottom if I had to jump off the vehicle to take cover. I remembered how I had failed the test in the boot camp swimming pool and nearly drowned. Now paranoia was beginning to creep in, and I became more and more fearful of what might happen. I felt like a target as I sat helplessly on top of the tracked vehicle waiting. "Hurry up and wait," I thought.

I searched for a possible escape route or form of protection should we come under attack, but there was none. To make matters worse, I was now carrying that 25 pound radio on my back. "Thanks Gordon, just what I need," I muttered to myself. It was ironic. The equipment that was supposed to protect me and my unit could easily take my life in this situation if I had to go into that water.

Finally, the vehicle lunged forward; and we came ashore behind the other vehicles. I quickly dismounted. We were instructed to form a single file as we prepared to move across a barren rice paddy into Dai Do. There was at least a thousand meters of open terrain to cross before we came under the cover of the village with its hedgerows and trees. I could see the remains of the village in the distance to the north.

As we began moving across the paddy, I saw holes and craters created by bombs and artillery from the battles that had been fought here a few days ago. I had never seen a bomb crater before. It was huge and uncanny looking – about 30 or more feet wide and 6 or 8 feet deep with water at the bottom. Clumps of dirt and boulders were strewn all around the lip of the hole. The smell of sulfur was evident from the high explosives that created the crater.

I thought of the destruction that such a weapon must be able to cause. I had seen movies of bombs exploding but had never been close to an actual air-strike. In the movies, there always seemed to be a big fireball, but you never really saw a crater, especially one this large.

"Hey Sergeant Gordon, what size bomb made this crater?" I asked.

"Probably a 500 pounder, maybe 250. Deadly stuff!"

"Yeah, ya' got that right!"

The thought of a jet streaking down from the sky with tons of death bolted beneath its wings made me thankful that the NVA didn't have such weapons to use against us.

About halfway across the paddy, the column came to a halt. The lead elements were now moving through the village. Everyone was quiet and cautious, anticipating the worst to come at any moment. It was like walking into an amusement park fun house and waiting for someone to come up behind you and shout "Boo!" You knew it was probably going to happen, but you didn't know when.

I knelt down next to a large mound of dirt. It was probably 20 feet wide and 5 feet tall. I thought that it might provide some protection if an attack were to come. A terrible stench hung heavy in the air here. What was that smell? Something rotten, like very spoiled food or meat.

A few other men took cover behind the dirt mound with me. We all maintained silence. Silence was good; you wanted to hear everything around you because sounds could quickly alert you to trouble.

The smell was starting to get to me. I had never smelled anything so awful in my life; yet I couldn't identify it or where it was coming from. I was beginning to feel nauseous.

Sweat ran down my cheek from the hundred degree heat. I removed one of my canteens to take a drink of water, hoping that it would help cool me down and take that horrible stench away. However, when I unscrewed the cap and took a swig, I was greeted with hot water, water almost hot enough to make coffee. The column began to move forward again, so I picked myself up preparing to move out.

"Hey man, did you see Charlie?"

"What? Charlie, Charlie who? What do you mean?" I didn't understand what Gordon was asking me.

"Charlie! The dead gook laying on the other side of the dirt mound," he said.

A dead NVA soldier lay on the ground on the opposite side of the dirt mound where I had taken shelter. Death, that was the stench that nearly took my breath away – death and decay.

This had been the enemy, one of the soldiers we were fighting. I was not prepared for the sight of that body. The man had fallen just a day or so before, probably killed by shrapnel from an exploding bomb or artillery. What was once a man's face was now a maggot infested hole. Flies had already laid eggs in his stomach wounds, and they had hatched into maggots in the rotting flesh as well.

It was impossible to tell how old the man was. He had been left behind by his comrades to rot in the sun. Would I be left someday to rot in this hell hole as this man had been, alone and far from home?

I moved away from the stench of death and tried to comprehend what I had just seen. I had been in country seven days now. I was sweltering from the heat, and I was entering a village where a fierce battle had been fought just days before. Last week, I had been back "in the world", a world so different from this one that you would think I was on a different planet.

As I entered the village, death was everywhere – dead Marines, dead NVA soldiers, dead animals, chickens, water buffalo. Was this real? It seemed like a nightmare that wouldn't end. As I walked cautiously forward, a dead NVA soldier lay on the ground in front of me. I saw no wounds on his body, and he wasn't rotting the way the other soldier had been. His eyes were open but looked nowhere.

I studied that body, trying to figure out why he was dead, how he had died. His feet were bare; then I saw that one of his heels had been completely blown away. He must have bled to death. Surely a wound like that would have been extremely painful making it impossible to escape.

In all my life, I had never seen so much death and destruction as I saw in Dai Do village. The village that was once the home of families and children now lay in ruin. This was not what I had imagined the war would be like. I saw more death that day than most people will see in a lifetime. My feelings about the war and our involvement in this conflict became feelings of indifference and my conviction became simply one of survival. I must survive this, nothing else mattered. I didn't care if we defeated the NVA, I didn't care if we won every battle, I didn't care if we suppressed

Communism. I only cared about surviving, one day at a time.

*Hut in Dai Do Village*

We moved deeper and deeper into the village now. At one point, I came upon a ditch. In it were the bodies of dozens of dead Marines. Some of our men were pulling the bodies out of the trench, one by one, and placing them in body bags to be evacuated and shipped back home to their next of kin. I counted 28 bodies in that ditch.

One body was right in front of me in this ditch. I needed to jump across and get to the other side. The man looked to be no older than I. His eyes were open and staring upward at nothing. I looked for the cause of his death. There were no visible wounds that I could see. His helmet was still on his head, but the chin strap was not buckled.

I leaped across the ditch. When I landed on the other side, my right foot slipped and kicked his head. His head tilted forward, and his helmet fell off. I felt ashamed that I had disturbed the dead Marine.

When his helmet fell off, I saw the wound that had killed him. A clean bullet hole was revealed in the back of his head, just below the area that would have been protected by his helmet. I thought about this for a moment. Had the Marine had his head tilted at a slightly different angle the moment the bullet had struck, the bullet might have grazed his helmet; and he might still be alive. Just the position of his body determined his fate that day in May. It was ironic to think that such a simple thing could decide whether you would live or die. That thought stuck in the back of my head from that point on. I didn't know it at the time, but it would decide my own fate six months later.

An enemy "pith helmet" was on the ground in front of me. Another Marine reached for the helmet, intending to take it as a souvenir.

Suddenly Gordon shouted, "Stop! Don't touch it, it could be booby trapped." It was a good thing I still had Gordon with me. He had been in country for almost 13 months now. He had experience, he knew things I needed to know; but soon he would be going home.

Booby traps – we had been taught some things about booby traps in jungle training. It seems the NVA liked to use anything that might entice a U.S. soldier to do something ordinary, like pick up a pith helmet for a souvenir. Had the helmet been booby trapped, it would probably have had an armed grenade under it or a thin trip wire to a grenade in a tin can. It would have come out of the can when the helmet was picked up.

The man still wanted that helmet so he looked around for a stick of some kind to put him at length from the helmet when he moved it. It was almost comical to watch as he stooped low and poked at the helmet with a long branch from a splintered tree. He'd poke at it and quickly duck, turning his head as though that would protect him if the helmet blew up. Then, he'd poke it again and repeat the process. Finally, he muttered a few obscenities, dropped the stick, and just grabbed the helmet from the ground. I started to duck myself when he did this, but nothing happened. He had his souvenir.

Our column stopped now, and an aerial observer appeared overhead. Gordon said it was an O-1 Cessna (Bird Dog). This was a Marine aircraft that often flew reconnaissance for ground units. The Bird Dog could fly slowly enough to allow the pilot good capabilities to spot enemy positions below. When the pilot spotted a target, he would radio the one four man, notify him of the target, and ask what type of ordinance might be allowable based on the location of friendly ground troops. It was important that the pilot know exactly where all friendly ground troops were so that the proper ordinance was used, and it was the one four man's responsibility to keep the pilot informed.

Often, the one four man would be required to reveal his position to this aerial observer. Revealing his position could prove dangerous to the one four man as well as his unit. So to protect himself from enemy detection, the one four man would use a signal mirror.

The mirror was used to flash the pilot and to indicate the unit's position in relationship to his. Because the mirror was reflecting the sun at the pilot only, it was not possible for the enemy to detect the one four man's position.

To tell the pilot where he was, the one four man would describe his position using the numbers on a clock. For example, if the one four man said, "I am at your two o'clock." This would mean that, if the pilot looked slightly to his right and down, he would have a general idea in what direction the one four man was in relationship to himself. The twelve o'clock position would be straight ahead for the pilot, and the six o'clock position would be behind him.

It was clear that there was still much to learn to be the one four man of a Marine line company. I was trying to soak in everything that Gordon explained to me; but I knew that, until I had to actually use what he had taught me, it was not going to truly sink in.

An hour had passed when jets appeared overhead. Gordon said they were F-4 Phantoms. As the jets circled, the AO fired a rocket into the village far ahead of us. When it exploded, a white plume of smoke rose. Gordon said it was a "Willie Pete" rocket (white phosphorous). These rockets could kill a person from the burning phosphorous but were used primarily to mark a target for the jets.

Seconds later, the jets came plummeting towards the earth heading for the area marked by the Willie Pete. They were fairly low when the first jet dropped two large, silvery canisters of napalm. They tumbled to earth and exploded seconds later in two huge balls of fire.

Right behind the first jet came the second jet, dropping six snake eyes. There were six tremendous explosions. You could feel the shock wave in the air, and the ground shook. Large plumes of dirt and black dust rose above the village in front of us where the bombs had impacted.

Even though we were at least a thousand meters from the explosion, shrapnel could be heard piercing the air as it was hurled hundreds of meters outward from the point of impact. The sound was similar to the ricocheting bullet you used to hear in old westerns, but amplified due to the size of the pieces. I could not imagine being at the receiving end of such fire power and surviving. If anyone had been alive at the target point when the napalm and bombs were dropped, they would surely be dead now.

Gordon said the combination drop of "snake and nape" was common. The first jet would drop the napalm which would cause the "gooks to get up and run" from the fireball. Then, the second jet would drop the 250 pound snake eyes while the "gooks were in the open, killing them all." This proved to be a very effective and lethal combination.

After the air-strike was over and things had settled down, the column moved out again. At one point, we came across a captain and a gunnery sergeant; probably the C.O. and 1st sergeant. Both were tied up in trees, their arms tied behind their backs. Both had been shot in the back of their heads.

Evidently, the company had been overrun. These men had been taken prisoner, probably tortured and then murdered. The NVA were a brutal enemy and took no mercy on captured soldiers.

From what I could learn, 2/4 had been sent to investigate intelligence reports of enemy activity in and around Dai Do. When they entered the village, the NVA sprang an ambush. The NVA had built fortified bunkers and tunnels throughout the village along strategic hedgerows. The enemy were protected while the Marines were in the open. Marine casualties were high, as the scenes I had just witnessed were clear evidence.

We soon reached the area where the napalm and bombs had been dropped. Huge craters littered the ground. Everything around the area was burnt. Large globs of the burnt napalm lay around the ground, stuck to shattered trees. Debris was everywhere.

We were told that this would be our CP (command post) for the night. I dropped my gear on the ground and took another drink of hot water. I was drenched in sweat from the heat and the weight of the load I had been carrying.

All around me, everyone started digging foxholes. It dawned on me that my preparatory training had not even taught me how to dig a foxhole. Not wanting to appear stupid, I took out my entrenching tool (a small folding shovel) and began to dig.

The entrenching tool has a handle about two feet long. The small shovel end folds and is typically used folded at a ninety degree angle to the handle. The shovel has a pointed blade and, when swung like a pick, works very effectively at digging. You could swing it with just one hand due to its compact size. The ninety degree angle of the shovel portion could not only work like a pick but was very useful in scooping the dirt up.

*Entrenching Tool*

The entire company was digging in for the night. A line of foxholes were dug in a large circle around the CP. I was a part of the Battalion CP which included the battalion commander (CO), who was a lieutenant colonel, the executive officer (XO), who was a major, and various other officers and enlisted men. A second company CP was nearby. The company CP consisted of the commanding officer, usually a captain, the 1st sergeant, who was usually a gunnery sergeant, the CO's radio operator, the one four man, and various other enlisted men. Each company also had a 60 millimeter mortar crew with several mortar tubes, and the battalion CP had an 81 millimeter mortar crew with tubes.

Mortars are a portable weapon. A battalion CP would contain 8 mortar tubes and perhaps 100 rounds of ammunition. The tubes, their mounting plates and the ammunition all had to be carried by the mortar crew. A mortar crew usually consisted of 5 men. Because of their size and weight, 81 mortars were kept at the battalion CP which was not as mobile as a company. They could be fired in support of the companies operating around the battalion. The 60 millimeter mortar was a similar but smaller weapon, lighter in weight, thus making it more mobile.

Each company as well as the battalion had a mortar and artillery FO, or forward observer. These men were usually enlisted men but could be officers as well. They were responsible for directing mortar and artillery missions in support of the unit. Because we were operating in an area close to the sea, the FO's could also direct naval gunfire from battleships offshore.

I was beginning to understand some of the basics of how a Marine unit would function in the field. Whenever a company would dig in, the grunts would dig foxholes forming a circle around the CP. The grunts would lay claymore mines and trip flares outside the perimeter of these lines. The flares would alert them if any enemy approached their lines in the dark. The claymore mines could then be set off by the Marines using a special detonator that was wired to the mine. The mines were usually placed 100 meters or so in front of the line, and the wire attached to it ran back to the line where it was attached to the detonator.

These mines would spray the enemy with a shower of large metal balls. These balls were usually lethal within 50 meters but could still wound an enemy solder up to 250 meters in front of the mine.

*Claymore Mine – Photo courtesy of Wikimedia.org*

Knowing that I had men forming a perimeter around me and that they were well armed gave me a feeling of security.

Exhausted, hot and inexperienced, I dug only a shallow foxhole and called it a day. I was hungry and wanted to rest. Since I had men all around me as protection, I saw no reason to exhaust myself any further by digging a large hole, which I probably would never need to use in the first place.

As night fell, it became quiet. Keeping noise and light to a minimum was imperative in order not to give your position away to the enemy. This was just fine with me as I wanted to get some sleep. Although I was not accustomed to sleeping on the bare ground in my clothes and boots, I soon drifted off to sleep from sheer exhaustion.

I don't know what time it was when the shelling started because I didn't hear the first rounds that were fired. But I was shocked awake when they exploded. The startled feeling was similar to the feeling I got in boot camp when the drill instructor woke us up by beating a baton inside a large metal trash can. It sent a feeling through my body like a jolt of electricity. The adrenaline in me went from zero to maximum.

My first thought was that foxhole I had dug earlier. I instinctively knew that I needed to find cover from the exploding rounds. Because of my haste to dig the hole, I found that my body would not fit into it. The hole was more like a very small crater than an actual foxhole.

I curled up into a fetal position trying to squeeze my body into the hole for protection. Then, I saw a flash in the northern sky like lightening, and seconds later I heard a very distinctive pop. A 130 millimeter artillery piece in the DMZ was firing an artillery round directly at us.

Approximately 10 to 15 seconds later, I heard the screaming freight train sound of the incoming round and, immediately afterwards, the loud explosion nearby. Fortunately for me the round did not impact in the CP, but it was certainly frightening to hear the sounds of incoming artillery being fired from miles away, directly at us.

The NVA fired only a few rounds because they did not want to give away their position. At night, the muzzle flash of the artillery piece firing could be easily seen. These rounds were meant to harass us and keep us awake and on our guard against a possible enemy ground attack.

After the firing had stopped, I went back to digging my foxhole much deeper, even though it was dark. I did not want to get caught again without the protection it could provide me. I had learned a valuable lesson that night and was thankful that I had survived my first enemy artillery attack.

The next morning, we packed up our gear and continued our sweep through Dai Do. The scene was much the same as the day before – bunkers, bomb craters, debris, shattered straw huts, enemy equipment, Marine equipment, and of course, the dead.

By midday, we had reached the end of the village. Except for the few rounds of artillery the night before, we had encountered no resistance and had not engaged the enemy in a firefight. It appeared that the NVA had left this area, but I assumed that they were probably still close by.

A new perimeter was formed, and we dug in for the night. The grunts went about putting out flares and claymores. The battalion 81 mortar crew began digging pits for their tubes. I quickly began work digging my new foxhole. I was not going to get caught out in the open tonight if we started taking incoming artillery again.

Shortly after dark the northern sky lit up for an instant, and I heard the gun pop. I grabbed my radio and jumped into my foxhole. Seconds later another man jumped into the hole with me. I didn't know who he was; it was too dark to tell.

The freight train sound of the incoming round flew overhead impacting somewhere to the south of us at least a few hundred meters away.

"I'm not getting out of this hole," he said.

"Neither am I," I replied.

"Candy Tuff one four, this is Blue Devil one four, over."

The regimental one four man was calling me on the radio.

"Wait one, Blue Devil, over." I replied.

"Candy Tuff one four, this is Blue Devil one four. I have a weather report for you, over."

"Wait one, Blue Devil, out."

I couldn't believe it. We were in the middle of an artillery attack and this guy was trying to give me a weather report. Don't waste my time. I already know what the weather is going to be tomorrow – hot, just like today, just like yesterday, just like every day in the Nam.

"Candy Tuff one four, this is Blue Devil one four. High temperature, 130, winds from the south, sunny with zero percent chance of rain."

"Roger, out." I replied as another round exploded inside our lines.

"Candy Tuff one four, do you copy, over?"

"I said roger, out."

Radio procedure was one thing I did learn in radio/telegraph school. I wanted to tell this guy that we were taking incoming but could not because the enemy monitored our radio transmissions. Revealing this would tell the enemy that he was right on target.

Finally, the incoming ceased. Things became deathly quiet again. I just sat there in the foxhole, shoulder to shoulder with the other Marine who had jumped in with me. I drifted off to sleep.

A few hours later, I was awakened by an intense volley of small weapons fire from our lines. A trip flare had been set off, and every man on the line in that area opened fire with his M-16. An M-60 machine gun crew also opened fire spraying the area around the flare, a wall of small arms fire. My immediate thought was that we were under a ground attack.

Moments later, the flare went out. Shouts rang out to cease fire. I learned the next day that a chicken in the village had tripped the flare. "Bet some grunts will have a good meal today," I muttered to myself.

When day finally broke, I crawled out of the foxhole, stiff from the awkward position I had to sleep in. The other Marine also crawled out, and I was surprised to see that it was the battalion XO, a major. He hurried off to talk to the battalion commander, Colonel Jarvas.

After a quick morning breakfast of C-rations, I was told that Bravo Company would be moving out heading east to an adjacent village. Only the battalion CP was staying behind with the 81 mortar crew, officers, and a few enlisted men. Now we had no one protecting us.

Gordon took over radio watch, and I just hung around – hurry up and wait as usual. Around mid morning, an aerial observer came on station; and Gordon turned the radio over to me. Basically I was to monitor the radio because the Bravo one four man was controlling the situation.

Bravo Company approached the village cautiously. They were no more than 20 or 30 meters away before the ambush was set off.

The NVA were dug in behind a hedgerow that surrounded the village. Automatic and small arms fire erupted, without warning, sending the Marines to the ground with only a few low paddy dykes as protection against the wall of bullets that was shredding their ranks. Soon mortars were exploding all around them, quickly inflicting heavy casualties.

"Candy Tuff one four, this is Bulldozer X-ray. Put your six on the line, over."

"Candy Tuff one four, do you copy, over."

The aerial observer was calling me. Why would he be calling me? What do I do? Where's Gordon. I couldn't find Gordon.

"Candy Tuff one four, get your six, now!" The aerial observer repeated.

"Sir, I don't understand, I'm new in country, over."

What did he mean by "get your six?" I didn't understand and the urgency in his voice was now causing my adrenaline to rush. Explosions, small arms fire, the situation was deteriorating rapidly.

"Put the Colonel on the radio son, now!"

"Roger, wait one." I replied.

I ran to the Colonel and handed him the receiver. "Sir, the AO wants to speak to you."

"Six, this is Bulldozer X-ray. Get your people back now! You're in imminent danger of being overrun. I've got waves of gooks coming from the back of the village charging forward towards your lines."

Colonel Jarvas turned to me and said, "Marine, get on line now and shoot anything that moves. Pass the word to every available man to get on line and shoot anything that moves."

Suddenly, we were in a desperate situation. Bravo Company, which was advancing on the village adjacent to us, was pinned down in the middle of the rice paddy and could be overrun by attacking NVA at any minute. If they were overrun, there would be no one between us and the enemy. Not only was Bravo Company in serious danger, but so was the entire battalion CP.

I moved to a bomb crater and took up my firing position. I locked and loaded a round into the chamber of my M-16 and flipped the safety switch off. I took several grenades from my shoulder belt and placed them on the ground in front of me.

Would my weapon even work? I had only been in country a few days and had never even fired it. I was scared to death. I knew I was trained well on firing the weapon and had qualified in boot camp as a rifle sharpshooter. But I had never fired my weapon at another human being. My job was a radio operator, not a grunt. I was certain that this would be my last day in the Nam, my last day on earth.

I could see people moving far in the distance; but they were just specs, indiscernible as friend or enemy. I did not want to shoot at anyone unless I was certain that I could identify him as the enemy.

The firefight was intense and Bravo Company was fighting hard to take control of the battlefield. Artillery was impacting in the village, and our 81 mortar crew was busy firing mortars into it as well.

Soon, choppers appeared overhead, CH-46's and F-4 Phantoms. The aerial observer was working with the Bravo one four man to drop snake and nape on the village.

"Bulldozer X-ray, use a run in heading of zero five zero, over."

The Bravo one four man had told the aerial observer to have the jets follow a heading of zero five zero when they dropped their bombs. You always wanted the fixed-wing to approach the target parallel to your troops so that, if the bombs overshot the target, they wouldn't be dropped on your own men.

Moments later, the jets came screaming down to earth at over 250 miles per hour and unleashed the napalm and snake eye bombs. The explosive power of these weapons gave the pinned-down Marines a chance to pull back from the engagement as the NVA took shelter in their fortified bunkers.

The Bravo one four man had executed a coordinated maneuver. Just after the napalm and bombs had exploded, the choppers began their descent into the rice paddy bringing dozens of reinforcements to assist the company and to take out the dead and wounded.

I looked out over the rim of the bomb crater and witnessed the chain of events unfolding in front of me. Two choppers about 20 meters above the ground suddenly dropped, shot down by enemy fire. As one struck the ground, it toppled over to its side. The other managed to stay upright. The Marines quickly struggled out of the downed choppers. Moments later the one that toppled over exploded in a ball of fire.

Our 81 mortar team was busy dropping round after round into the village. Now a pair of Huey gunships appeared overhead.

"Bulldozer X-ray, this is Whiskey Delta. What have you got for us, over?"

"Ah, roger, Whiskey Delta, we've got gooks in the open. Marking the target now. Run in zero five zero. Use everything you've got."

The aerial observer fired his Willy Pete rocket which exploded in a cloud of white somewhere inside the village. Immediately afterwards, the pair of Hueys approached the village, one behind the other. The first chopper unleashed a volley of 60 millimeter rockets as all six of his M-60 machine guns fired continuously.

I was witnessing a ferocious battle just a thousand meters in front of me. I caught all of the radio traffic between the Bravo one four man and the air support he had summoned. The attacks were all coordinated just as a conductor would conduct an orchestra, in unison, with precision.

While the choppers were making their attacks, the mortar crew continued to fire mortars into the forward lines of the enemy, the hedgerows where the ambush was sprung. The chopper attacks were deeper inside the village, and the run-in heading was chosen so that our men would remain out of the line of fire while still providing safety to the choppers from the mortar attack. I was amazed at the amount of firepower we were putting into the village.

The reinforcement choppers were dropping another company to aid Bravo, and we surely were gaining the upper hand in this battle. They landed in the northwest corner of the rice paddy, so they would not be affected by our mortar attack. As the choppers came in, one after another, the Huey's continued to circle the village and attack in a coordinated manner.

Without warning, the entrenched NVA moved from their fixed positions and began a counterattack moving into the open rice paddy. Bravo Company and its reinforcements had formed a firing line out in the rice paddy taking cover behind the paddy dikes.

Waves of NVA were pouring out of the village and into the open, attacking the line of Marines and trying to overrun their position. If that happened, I would surely have to take up the fight to protect the battalion CP.

I tightened my grip on my M-16 and took aim in the field in front of me. The adrenaline raced through my body as the fear of dying almost overwhelmed me. This was it, real combat, nothing like the war movies I had seen but the real thing.

It seemed like mass confusion in front of me. The Hueys were strafing the NVA with machine gun fire and rockets; hand grenades were exploding in the middle of the NVA attackers. The troops on the ground that were under attack were firing with intensity and were nearly engaged hand to hand.

It seemed like a suicide attack by the NVA. As I look back on that day in May now, I guess the strategy of the NVA was to try to overwhelm the Marines with numbers, hoping that the mass attack would scare the Marines and cause their lines to break. I recall hearing a radio transmission from the aerial observer that it looked like one of the mass attacks the North Koreans had tried to launch against the Marines in the Korean War.

The NVA counterattack quickly faded; our firepower was too intense and the enemy soon began to retreat back into the cover of the village. Once again, death covered the ground.

Colonel Jarvas had decided to hold in place. The battle subsided, and the NVA ceased to fire on the Marines in the rice paddy.

The aerial observer continued to circle overhead peering down into the village and observing the movement of the enemy. The choppers had left, and the reinforcements were now in place with Bravo Company.

"One four man up!" The 81 mortar crew had run out of ammunition, and I was being summoned to call in some resupply choppers. We needed mortars, ammo, water and other supplies. We needed to get the dead and wounded Marines onto medivac choppers.

Gordon told me what to do, and I called regiment on the radio asking for the resupplies and medivac choppers. Then, Gordon took over radio watch; and I went back to my foxhole. I decided to dig it a little bit deeper, just to play it safe.

Resupply choppers landed in an open area to the west of me, coordinated by Gordon. Marines carried body bags to the Landing Zone (LZ); and wounded Marines, some helped by others, limped and walked to the LZ to await medivac to Dong Ha or Quang Tri where they would receive better medical treatment for their wounds.

For the remainder of the day, artillery and air power worked the village. The artillery FO's and Bravo company one four man did their jobs. By dusk, the village lay in complete ruin.

The Marines in the rice paddy were pulled back to Dai Do just before dark, where they dug in for the night forming a tight perimeter around the battalion CP. I met the Bravo one four man, a lance corporal. He had done a magnificent job that day coordinating the air attacks and air lift of reinforcements.

As the day drew to an end, we sat around cooking C-rations and talking about the events of that day. I was fortunate; I had not participated in the battle that day. I had only been an observer, but I had witnessed the use of coordinated air and ground fire against a well-entrenched enemy. I had listened to the radio exchanges between the ground one four man and the supporting aircraft. It was the best OJT I could get, sitting a thousand meters away from all the action yet able to see and hear everything first hand.

That night the village was bombarded with artillery fire of all sizes, constantly, all night long. I slept a few hours but found it difficult to do so with all of the noise from the guns and the explosions nearby. I also feared a counterattack, but none came.

The next day, we packed up all our gear and moved out across the rice paddy towards the village which had been the scene of that fierce battle the day before. The enemy had fled during the night, pulling back to the north, towards the DMZ. Dai Do and its surrounding villages were about six miles south of the DMZ.

The scene in the abandoned village was a familiar one, but this time there were no dead Marines in the village. This would be the last we would see of the 320th NVA Division for a while. For now, the worst was over; and so was my first week in Vietnam. I had survived my first week and my first taste of combat. Survival would become my motivation and all that would matter to me in the months ahead.

The battle of Dai Do had earned the entire 3rd Marine Regiment a Navy Unit Commendation. Although 1/3 had not seen the most intense fighting of the battle, it was an experience I will never forget. For the next several days we stayed in the village of Dai Do, while platoons patrolled the surrounding villages and hamlets.

During those days in Dai Do, food and ammunition were flown in to us on a routine basis. However, water was not. We had been instructed to fill our canteens from the village well. The well was located in the middle of an open rice paddy.

One day another Marine and I took our canteens out to the well to be refilled. I felt secure now that the battle of Dai Do was over and the enemy was moving back towards North Vietnam. So I did not carry my weapon or gas mask with me.

I had only filled one canteen when suddenly I sensed the faint presences of tear gas. My heart began to pound and the adrenaline flowed once again sending fear through my body. The gas intensified, and I began to panic. I had no weapon or gas mask with me, and I feared that the gas was a prelude to an attack. The other Marine must have had the same idea as we grabbed our canteens and ran as fast as we could, back to the village.

When we arrived, everyone gave us this strange look. We both looked like we had just seen a ghost. "What's with you guys?" another Marine asked. "We were just gassed!" I explained. "No you weren't, that was a training exercise, FNG!" Laughter broke out, and I felt like I had just made a fool of myself. I still had much to learn.

The next day the well seemed to have gone dry, which was unusual for a village well. The Colonel instructed some of the men to go down into the well on a rope to investigate. When one of the men emerged from the stone opening, his explanation of the problem was surprising as well as sickening.

At the bottom of the well, he had found a dead NVA soldier. Needless to say, by now it was a little too late to do anything about it. We had all drank the water that had been poisoned by the fleeing enemy. It wasn't long before most of us came down with dysentery. So they told us to get our water from a nearby stream that emptied into the Song Bo Dieu, that is, until a patrol found another dead NVA soldier upstream from where we were filling up. From then on, water was flown into us in a very large black rubber balloon with a valve on it (a water bladder).

The following is an excerpt taken from a publication I received after my return from Vietnam. The publication is called "The Fighting Third" and the article describes "The Battle of Dai Do: Seven Days in May."

_—–•—__–•—__–•—__–•—__–•—__–•—__–•—__–•—__–•—__–•—__–•—_

*"3rd Marine Division Leathernecks clashed with a large North Vietnamese Army force in seven days of bitter fighting last May near the village of Dai Do, just two miles north of Dong Ha...*

*Journal:*

*The battle started in the early morning hours of April 30th when a Navy utility landing craft (LCU), loaded with supplies enroute from Cua Viet to Dong Ha, was ambushed by the NVA.*

*Elements of the 2nd Bn., Fourth Marines, patrolling in the vicinity of the ambush, swung into action. They soon made contact with the enemy near the village of Dai Do, just two miles north of Dong Ha. The Marines became heavily engaged with the enemy force and by nightfall the entire battalion was in contact with the enemy.*

*Extremely heavy fighting broke out on the morning of May 1, the traditional communist holiday, when Marines tried to advance against the heavy enemy opposition in close range fighting. Later battlefield estimates determined the enemy force to be several regiments of NVA soldiers.*

*In describing the near hand-to-hand combat, which at times saw the opposing sides firing at point blank range, Colonel Milton A. Hull, commander of the Third Marines, explained, 'The NVA in this area has a unique technique. Hiding in rice paddies and hedgerows, he lets you advance right up to him before he engages you at very close range.'*

*Marines called in supporting air-strikes and artillery throughout May 1, and the communists withstood the barrage and by mid-afternoon launched a very heavy counterattack against the entire front of the Marine battalion. The men of 2/4 contained the counterattack and dug in for the night.*

*The next day fighting continued in much the same manner as on May 1. More artillery and air-strikes were called and 2/4 once again started to move against a strong and determined enemy force. May 2 once more saw the enemy launch a counterattack. The Marines held and hurled the enemy back and at nightfall dug in along the sandy terrain near the Cua Viet River. The fact that the entire battalion of Marines had been able to advance only some 2,000 meters during two days of bitter fighting testifies to the fierce battle and strong enemy resistance.*

*At daylight on May 3, 2/4 again rose to move against the enemy and the NVA again counterattacked. This was the third counterattack by hardcore NVA forces in four days.*

*Colonel Hull recalls, 'After three very hard counterattacks, $2^{nd}$ Battalion, Fourth Marines had suffered some casualties but their ranks were still well organized and they were full of motivation and wanted to continue the attack and drive the enemy back. However, I had a fresh unit at hand and thought that it was about time to give the battalion a little rest.'*

*The new unit, 1/3 was committed to action on May 4 to take over the area of responsibility vacated by Leathernecks from the Fourth Marines.*

*At this time it was learned that the enemy force in the area above the Cua Viet River consisted of two regiments from the $320^{th}$ NVA Division. To aid Colonel Hull's Marines in their battle against this large NVA force, the Army's $3^{rd}$ Battalion of the $21^{st}$ Light Infantry Brigade was deployed in the third Marines Tactical Area of Responsibility (TAOR).*

*On May 5, 1/3 continued to pursue the enemy force and prevented the NVA from reaching its objective, the Cua Viet River. The fresh Marine battalion made rapid advances against the enemy during the morning and early afternoon. But by late afternoon the enemy regrouped and counter attacked once more.*

*This, the last of the enemy's counterattacks, was an en-masse attack similar to those used by the North Koreans during the fighting in the early 1950's. Colonel Hull later described the attack as 'a vicious counterattack with charges by NVA soldier's running at the Marines and firing automatic weapons from the hip and from the shoulder at very close range.'*

*But the attack was again contained and the Marines held their ground.*

*For the next three days artillery and air-strikes continued to hit the now fleeing enemy as more forces were called in to help drive them from the terrain along the Cua Viet.*

*The 1$^{st}$ Battalion of the Army's Fifth Cavalry was called in to harass the North Vietnamese as they fled towards the DMZ.*

*By the end of the first seven days in May the enemy toll stood at 1,069 confirmed NVA dead. Scattered action in the days that followed pushed the final total to1,800. In addition, the fleeing enemy left behind 150 individual weapons, 49 crew served weapons and several hundred rounds of small arms ammunition and other field gear."*

—-•—-—-•—-—-•—-—-•—-—-•—-—-•—-—-•—-—-•—-—-•—-—-•—-—-•—-—-•—-

The following is a copy of the Navy Unit Commendation awarded to our Regiment for the battle of Dai Do.

—-•—-—-•—-—-•—-—-•—-—-•—-—-•—-—-•—-—-•—-—-•—-—-•—-—-•—-—-•—-

*"WASHINGTON*

*The Secretary of the Navy takes pleasure in presenting the NAVY UNIT COMMENDATION to*

*THIRD MARINE REGIMENT, THIRD MARINE DIVISION (REIN), FMF*

*For service as set forth in the following*

*CITATION:*

*For exceptionally meritorious and heroic achievement during the period 30 April to 16 May 1968 while engaged in combat against enemy forces in southeastern Cam Lo*

*District, Quang Tri Province, Republic of Vietnam. Initiating counteraction against a numerically superior enemy force in the vicinity of Dai Do and along the strategically critical Thach Han River, the Third Marine Regiment demonstrated an outstandingly high degree of combat readiness and aggressiveness during a series of fiercely fought and bitterly opposed combat actions. In the face of heavy enemy small arms, mortars and artillery fire, the Third Marine Regiment moved relentlessly forward and surmounted every obstacle to inflict over 1500 casualties upon the enemy and capture large quantities of weapons and ammunition. The success achieved by the regiment and its attached Army and Air Force units precluded the closing of the Thach Han River – a communication and resupply route essential to units in the Northern I Corps area – and prevented the enemy from attacking and isolating the cities of Dong Ha and Quang Tri and their respective military complexes. By their valiant fighting spirit, efficient teamwork, professionalism, and dedication, the officers and men of the Third Marine Regiment and attached units achieved a resounding victory over the enemy and contributed essentially to the United States efforts in Southeast Asia. Their inspiring performance reflected great credit upon themselves and the Marine Corps, and was in keeping with the highest traditions of the United States Armed Forces.*

*Secretary of the Navy"*

*Enemy Bunker in Dai Do Village*

*Talking to the Aerial Observer*

# CHAPTER

# *SEVEN*

## THE VILLAGE OF LAI AN

After the battle of Dai Do, things became peaceful for a while. Without the pressures of combat, I was able to learn enough about tactical air control to take over the job as one four man for Alpha Company. Every day, I would go on patrols with a platoon. Because of the enemy activity in the days past, I utilized an aerial observer to search ahead of the platoon in the various villages and hamlets that we patrolled.

The peace wasn't to last very long, though. On May 27, we received orders to move out again. We left at night in total darkness, without the light of a full moon. It was to our advantage to move at such times, because there would be less chance of detection by the enemy.

We were heading north towards the DMZ. We walked all night, approximately six miles, through rice paddies which were now filled with six or eight inches of water.

I was carrying my normal load of equipment – the 25 pound radio, 2 spare batteries, 5 days worth of canned C-rations, a poncho, an entrenching tool, extra socks, insulated poncho liner, my M-16, 4 canteens of water (each holding one quart of water when full), my bayonet, 2 bandoliers of ammunition, 6 fully loaded magazines of ammunition, 4 smoke grenades, 2 hand grenades, a map, a compass, pencil, paper and envelopes (to write home with), my helmet, flak jacket and, of course, the clothes I wore. In all, the load I carried weighed approximately 75 pounds.

*Carrying a normal load*

We reached our objective just before dawn, within a few thousand meters of the DMZ and the Ben Hai River. We were near the ocean, and the terrain here was flat with little vegetation or trees. The rice paddies here were dry.

As we walked through a rice paddy, I could hear bullets zipping past me, stray bullets from the fighting that had broken out ahead of us. Our lead elements were already engaged in a firefight. I ducked each time I heard a bullet, a futile but instinctive reaction; because once you've heard that zipping sound, it has already flown past you.

The company CP stopped in an area of small, dried-up rice paddies and hedgerows. Bravo Company was in the lead, and we were holding our position while they engaged the enemy. I found some cover in a small trench.

As I monitored the radio, I heard the Bravo one four man call battalion requesting an aerial observer. Soon an O-1 was flying overhead forward of my position.

The fighting went on all day long. At times F-4 Phantoms dropped snake and nape a thousand meters or so just north of Bravo. I listened to my radio to see if I was going to be needed, but Bravo one four had full control of the air support that day.

At one point the Bravo one four called me, and I thought for a moment that I was going to get into the firefight. Bravo one four had just had his thumb shot off, his second wound since he had arrived in country four months ago. He said the pain was unbearable, but he wasn't going to have himself medivaced; his company needed him.

Two wounds in four months – I was actually envious. Two wounds in a single tour of duty meant that, when this firefight was over, Bravo one four would be sent to the rear where he would spend the remainder of his tour. The "rear" was Quang Tri, Battalion Headquarters where there were hot food, cots to sleep on, showers, and sand bag bunkers for protection. Now all he had to do was survive the firefight.

The day dragged on, and there was little I could do but hurry up and wait. I dropped my gear and stayed close to the Company CO in case he needed me. As the day drew to an end, the CO told us to dig in, and we would hold our current position for the night. I had to call in a resupply chopper to bring us food, water, and ammunition.

With that done, I focused on digging a new foxhole. With the experience of Dai Do behind me, I was becoming proficient at digging it. I dropped all my gear, including my helmet and flak jacket, and took out the entrenching tool to start digging.

As I was digging in for the night, men from the platoons were coming into the company CP to pick up ammunition, food, and water. There was a lot of activity in the CP due to this distribution of supplies. I didn't think much about it at the time, because I was still new in country; but such activity clearly identified the company CP. That meant we were soon to become a target for the NVA which Bravo Company had been fighting earlier in the day.

Apparently, the NVA had a forward observer who could see the activity in our CP. The terrain in this area provided some high ground where some small hills stood out. It was solid soil, which meant the possibility of bunkers and tunnels. I had been told that the NVA were proficient at digging tunnels connecting their bunkers, allowing them to move around their position underground, without detection. Through these tunnels, it was even possible for the enemy to move undetected inside our lines. Openings into the tunnels were well-camouflaged.

My foxhole was about 8 to 10 inches deep when the round exploded in the middle of our CP. I never heard the tube pop or the round coming. It was a 60 millimeter mortar.

"Corpsman up!" someone yelled.

I hit the ground inside my shallow foxhole expecting more rounds to start impacting. When I hit the ground, I felt a pain in my left shoulder but brushed it off, thinking it was merely the way I had hit the ground. I lay there for several minutes waiting for something else to happen, but nothing did.

I didn't pay much attention to things going on around me. Some men had been hit from the exploding mortar, but none was seriously injured. I just concentrated on getting my foxhole dug and worked frantically at the task.

"Hey man, you've been hit." The corpsman was making rounds checking people out.

"What? Where?" I asked.

"In the shoulder. Take your shirt off, and let me take a look."

My shirt was bloody at the shoulder. The pain I had felt when I hit the ground was from the wound. I had taken three pieces of shrapnel in the left shoulder from the exploding mortar.

The doc wiped the wound off with alcohol and then used his hemostats to remove three small pieces of shrapnel. Each was about the size of a pencil eraser, certainly not a wound that I was worried about. I did not know that these wounds would qualify me for the Purple Heart medal until I returned to the rear a year later. It was handed to me as I left Vietnam.

Twelve men had been wounded from that one round. Fortunately, no one had been seriously wounded; and no one needed to be medivaced. The activity in our CP was quickly reduced to prevent more injuries should the NVA attack us again.

I spent the night in my foxhole. Given the events of the day and the fact that I had been wounded, I did not want to take any more chances. We were very close to the DMZ, which meant that we were within range of the larger NVA guns that had fired at us when we were in Dai Do village.

The next morning, Alpha Company took over the point of our position. Bravo Company moved to the west of us. Lead elements of Alpha Company moved into the open. I was approximately 100 meters back from the lead elements with the company commander and other men in the CP.

As soon as our forward lines began to advance into the open, the fighting broke out again. We were receiving heavy machine gun fire from NVA entrenched in bunkers north of us.

I hit the ground behind a rice paddy dike. It was difficult to crawl forward with all of the equipment I was carrying. I looked over the rice paddy dike and saw another one 25 meters ahead. I decided to get up and run forward to it.

I stood up and took a few steps forward when suddenly bullets swept past me. They seemed to be zeroing in on me! I ran forward, zigzagging as I ran and saw dirt kicking up around me from the bullets.

When I dropped down to the ground behind the paddy dike, I realized why I was the personal target of some NVA soldier – I had my whip antenna on my radio and it was standing high above my head like a neon sign saying, "Shoot me, here I am." It made me feel foolish. One firefight was not enough experience to survive in the Nam. I still had much to learn.

I rolled over onto my back and slipped off the radio. I removed the whip antenna, folded it up, and stored it in the canvas pouch designed for it (which was attached to one side of the radio). I pulled the tape antenna from the pouch and installed it on the radio. Then, I called the battalion one four man for a radio check to see if he could hear me. Communications with battalion were fine, so I slipped the radio back on.

"One four man up!"

The CO was calling for me to move forward. Given the fact that I had been pegged by an NVA sniper, I did not want to move from my current position where I had some cover to hide behind.

"One four man up!"

"Shit!" I muttered to myself. There was no way I was going to get away with just lying here. The CO needed me, and I knew it was important.

I stood again and ran forward. Again, I could hear the bullets whizzing past me. Bullets were kicking up dirt around my feet as I ran another 25 meters. I dropped to the ground behind a large mound of dirt where the CO was taking cover with his radio operator.

"Hunt, I need an air-strike on those sand dunes," he said, pointing to an area northwest of our position.

I took out my map and asked the CO to show me where we were. I needed to get a fix on our position. The dunes were perhaps 600 meters from our position. Our forward lines were approximately 100 meters from our position. That meant 250 pound snake bombs and napalm could be safely used.

I told the CO to have our forward elements mark their positions with signal panel markers. These were colored panels about two feet square, used to show an aerial observer where the forward positions of friendly forces were. By knowing where our forward elements were, the AO could be certain not to direct the fixed-wing aircraft to drop their ordinance on friendly troops; and he could tell how much distance there was between friendly forces and the enemy target.

I called battalion on the radio. "Candy Tuff one four, this is Alpha one four, over."

"Alpha, Candy Tuff, over."

"Candy Tuff, I need an aerial observer ASAP, over."

"Roger, out." battalion replied.

Soon an O-1 was flying overhead. "Alpha one four, this is Spider Zulu, over."

"Spider Zulu, this is Alpha one four. I need snake and nape on enemy bunkers, coordinates one six three eight five seven. Friendlies to the south, marked by panels. Run in heading, zero seven five, over."

"Ah roger, Alpha. Snake and nape. I have your friendlies in sight, going in for a closer look."

The Cessna made a shallow dive in front of my position in the vicinity of the enemy bunkers. As he approached the area, I could hear enemy weapons firing up at him.

"Spider Zulu, you're taking fire, over."

The Cessna pulled up and to the north quickly to avoid the enemy fire.

"Alpha, I've got gooks in the open. Calling for snake and nape."

It took about 15 minutes before two F-4 Phantoms were circling overhead. The Cessna turned and approached the target on the run in heading I had given him. He fired one Willie Pete rocket which exploded in the midst of the enemy position.

"Alpha one four, how does that look, over?"

"Skipper, how does that look?" I asked the CO. The CO radioed his platoon leaders to be sure that our forward elements were far enough back from the marked target. Everything looked good.

"Spider Zulu, affirmative, over."

"Get your heads down," the AO replied. Within seconds, the first jet rolled in on the run in heading, swooping down from the sky. As he approached the target area, 4 canisters of napalm dropped from his wings and tumbled to earth exploding in 4 huge fireballs that blanketed the area in front of us for 500 meters or more. Right behind the first jet came the second, releasing eight 250 pound snake eye bombs. Eight powerful explosions followed in unison, shaking the ground and throwing dirt and shrapnel upward and outward.

The jets returned to their overhead position circling the area as the Cessna continued his observation below them. When the dust and fireball dissipated, I could see men in the distance, running. Wow! Is that the enemy? I grew excited that I could actually see the enemy running around in front of me meters away. I dropped to a prone position and lifted my M-16 to my shoulder taking aim. I wanted to "get me a kill"; but before I could fire, the CO knocked my M-16 from my shoulder and shouted, "That's not your job, Hunt. Those could be our own men. Don't ever do that again!" Gordon was right, my weapon was my radio; leave the close ground fighting to the grunts.

Pop! Suddenly I heard that distinct sound of an artillery gun firing at us from North Vietnam. "Incoming!" someone shouted. Pop! Pop! Pop! More guns fired; it must have been an entire battery. We all hit the ground instinctively waiting for that freight train sound of the incoming rounds. Seconds later the rounds impacted all around us. That adrenaline rush came again, and this time I knew what to do.

I radioed the aerial observer, "Spider Zulu, we're taking incoming from the north, over."

"Roger that, Alpha. Wait one." The Cessna turned north and headed for the Ben Hai River. We were extremely close to the river and North Vietnam.

Pop! Pop! Pop! The rounds kept coming. What started out to be a normal firefight was turning into another major battle. Small arms fire was erupting from our lines in front of me. The NVA had a certain advantage over us because they were dug in with bunkers to protect them while we were in the open.

The artillery FO had moved up to our position now and was calmly taking an azimuth with his compass to get the general direction of the incoming fire. By knowing the azimuth (direction) from which the artillery fire was coming, the AO could plot it on his map from our location and then have a general idea where to look for the guns.

"Hunt, tell your AO the azimuth is zero two five."

"Spider Zulu, azimuth zero two five from our position, over."

"Ah, roger. I've got the tubes in sight. Marking the target." The AO had spotted the tubes. Even though they were camouflaged and difficult to see, every time they fired, a puff of smoke would appear from each gun. I later learned that the guns were approximately six miles inside North Vietnam. The aerial observer was taking a great chance flying that far into North Vietnam, because he was in a very slow flying aircraft that could have been easily shot down by anti-aircraft guns.

The artillery barrage ceased, and I knew that the jets had dropped their remaining ordinance on those guns. Our lines had advanced forward and the CP was moving forward as well. I ran to keep up; but, with the radio and other equipment I was carrying, it was difficult. The heat was intense, and my muscles felt like rubber.

I ran from one paddy dike to another. There was a shrub line ahead, and I could see the CO and other men in the CP with him. They had stopped their forward advance, which gave me a chance to catch up.

The intense firing had stopped now, and only a sporadic shot could be heard now and then. We had taken the enemy position, and our troops were searching what was left of the enemy bunkers. I looked at my map and could see that we were in a village called Lai An.

One of the first things I had learned from Gordon was how to read a map. It was absolutely vital that I know where I was on a map at all times. This involved studying the terrain around me and identifying features that would help me pinpoint my position. I had to learn how to read the coordinates on the map, which was broken down into 1000 meter squares commonly called "clicks."

I was exhausted and took out a canteen to take a swig of the hot water. This had been the first real firefight in which I had been given the opportunity to do my job as a one four man. I had worked with an aerial observer, coordinated an airstrike, and aided in locating NVA artillery which was firing at us. I had "done good." I reflected upon the events of this operation, I felt I had crossed a hurdle and was no longer that FNG who had arrived in country less than a month ago.

"I need a cigarette!" I said. I didn't smoke. As a matter of fact, I had only smoked one cigarette in my entire life. (A couple of us skipped our last class in Junior High and snuck off into the woods to smoke. I gagged on the thing and decided then that cigarettes weren't for me.) Today was different though. I had come to the conclusion that, today, I had become a man. I had faced a combat situation, done my job helping to defeat the enemy and save men from what was becoming an overwhelming situation. I had earned my pay, all $235.00 (per month) of it; and I felt like celebrating.

The CO pulled out a pack of filterless Camel's, shook the pack to bring a cigarette out, and waved it in front of me. Camel's, wow, that was a real "man's" cigarette. I took one, and he lit it for me. I drew a puff and immediately choked on it, coughing the same way I had choked when I was that kid in Junior High. Everyone laughed, but I didn't care. I took another puff and did my best to keep from coughing again.

"Move out!" the CO yelled.

We had moved through the remains of the village and continued to move north towards the Ben Hai River. The closer we got to North Vietnam, the more likely we would take artillery incoming as well. The soil was sandy here, not good for digging a new foxhole. We settled down for the night in our new position.

The village was in rubble much like Dai Do had been. I had been told that air-strikes and naval gunfire had been directed into the village days before our arrival, to "prep" the area first. This was SOP (standard operating procedure) prior to entering a suspected enemy position.

There were no South Vietnamese civilians left in the village at the time of the prep. They had probably left long ago when the NVA had taken it over. As we swept through the village, some of the grunts looked for souvenirs. We came upon a few dead NVA soldiers, apparently killed in earlier fighting. The NVA leather belt with its brass buckle and red star was a popular souvenir among Marines. Weapons, helmets, and flags were all items of interest to souvenir hunters – something to take home and show friends and family. I had no interest in souvenirs or touching the dead. I couldn't help thinking that these men had been alive just hours earlier, fighting us, doing their job just as we had been doing our jobs. And it struck me that I was probably responsible for some of their deaths; I had directed that airstrike. I told myself, this was war; men killed or were killed themselves. That's just the way it was.

We were within 500 meters of the Ben Hai River now. I heard tubes pop again from deep inside North Vietnam.

"Incoming, incoming!" I shouted. I dove to the ground and, before I could call the aerial observer, he was calling me.

"Alpha one four, are you taking incoming again?" he asked.

"Roger that, over."

"I just saw the tubes pop again. Looks like we need work on those guns. Hang in there one four. I'm going to call in some naval gunfire."

Spider Zulu knew his job as well. I was glad to have him on station and just seconds away providing air support for us.

Out in the Gulf of Tonkin, naval ships with eight inch guns would soon be firing at the NVA artillery battery. It was fortunate that we were operating near the coast as these ships could not support us if we were further inland.

Pop! Pop! Pop! The guns continued to fire. There was no place to hide. We were out in the open, and the sandy soil made it impossible to dig any kind of hole for cover. I looked around me and saw a bomb crater nearby. Using the "low crawl" I had learned in infantry training, I crawled on my belly to the bomb crater. At least this put my body below ground level and provided some protection from flying shrapnel.

The shelling lasted another five minutes, but seemed like an eternity. When you are under an artillery barrage, your only thought is to make it stop. It's like a nightmare you can't wake up from, horrifying. First, you hear the tube pop, and then you count, five seconds, ten seconds, and sometimes longer, waiting for the round to impact. You know it's coming at you, but you don't know where it will hit. Then that freight train sound of the incoming round screams loudly just before it explodes.

I had been told earlier that the freight train sound was a good thing; because, if you heard it, the round had already passed your position. It is the round that gets you that you never hear, because it's coming right at you. That's a good thing, too, because you die without even knowing what's about to happen to you. Either way, incoming artillery scared the hell out of me; and I just wanted it to end.

"Corpsman up!" someone shouted. Someone had been hit by the incoming artillery.

"How would I ever survive a year of this?" I wondered. I had already been wounded and had only been here less than a month. The combat seemed to be constant, one battle after another. I knew men survived, did their tour of duty, and went home. But that day I was certainly not convinced that I would be one of those survivors.

The shelling stopped, finally. "One four man up!" Here we go again, someone needs me.

"One four man up!" I jumped up and ran towards the calling voice. It was the corpsman. He had a wounded Marine by his side.

"You the one four man?" he asked.

"Yeah, what do ya' need?" I replied.

"I need a priority medivac, I've got to get this man to a hospital ship immediately."

"Roger that. Candy Tuff one four, this is Alpha one four. Priority medivac, over."

I called battalion and requested a priority medivac. There were three terms used to describe the severity of a wounded soldier – routine, priority, and emergency. A routine medivac was used to describe a soldier who was either dead or not seriously wounded but needed additional treatment that the corpsman could not provide. A priority medivac meant a seriously wounded soldier who did not have life threatening wounds. Such wounds needed immediate treatment and possible surgery. The emergency medivac was a life threatening situation that required immediate surgery to save the man's life.

The type of medivac determined how quickly you would get a chopper to take the wounded out. For routine medivac's, the chopper might not come for hours, depending on availability. A priority medivac chopper usually came within 30 minutes or as soon as the first available chopper could be sent.

The emergency medivac was the most important of the three, and only the corpsman or battalion doctor could request such a medivac. This medivac chopper came almost immediately and was often any available helicopter within radio range and already in the air on another mission. If that mission was not an emergency, he was diverted immediately. However, an even more serious request was the emergency medivac with AMA (airborne medical assistance). This meant that a doctor had to be onboard the chopper. The wounds were so serious that even the delay to transport the wounded man could cost him his life. These choppers were on standby 24 hours a day and could be airborne and enroute within seconds.

"Alpha one four, this is Whiskey Bravo, inbound. What is your position, over?"

Where were we? I pulled my map from my pocket and unfolded it across my lap, as I dropped down on one knee.

"Roger Whiskey Bravo, grid square one four eight five. I'm at your two o'clock, over."

"What are you doing so far north? I've never flown this far north before. Is LZ secure, over?"

"Whiskey Bravo, this is Alpha one four, popping smoke, over." I answered, evading his questions about the LZ being secure. It was very open terrain, no trees to worry about, which made landing a helicopter just about anywhere possible. That was not always the case as I would later find out.

An Army chopper approached. No wonder he was having reservations. The Army didn't usually provide air support to us; but since this was a priority medivac, he must have been the next available chopper. A Marine chopper wouldn't have questioned the safety of the LZ.

As the chopper approached, that adrenaline fear swept through me again. What was I thinking? We were just a few hundred meters from North Vietnam, had just taken incoming artillery moments ago; and I was popping a smoke grenade that told any NVA FO precisely where I was, not to mention the target the chopper provided for those NVA guns.

The Huey landed; the noise was so intense from his rotors that it was impossible to hear anything. Dirt and sand kicked up in the air along with all kinds of debris, and I had to cover my eyes to keep from being blinded.

The corpsman and another Marine helped put the wounded man into the chopper, and minutes later he had lifted off and was heading south. I was relieved that this episode was over and listened intently for that familiar "pop" sound from incoming artillery. Fortunately, it didn't come.

As the day came to an end, so did our movement. We had accomplished our mission, cleared the area of the enemy, gathered intelligence, and killed numerous NVA troops. The enemy force we had been fighting was part of the 320th NVA Division that we had fought a month ago in Dai Do.

Just before dusk, we received the order to pull back. That night we marched the six miles we had covered a few nights earlier, back to the Cua Viet River. It would be another sleepless night for us, as we humped back to our base camp area on the Cua Viet. Hot, hungry and exhausted, we walked through the rice paddies filled with water once again, hoping we would not have any more encounters with the enemy. It would be good to get back to friendly territory and to get some down time for rest and relaxation.

By daybreak, we had reached the river. The company took up a position in a small village on the south side of it. We spent several days in the village, which was a welcome change to my first 30 days in the Nam. We swam in the river every day to cool down; there was no shooting, no artillery, and no enemy threats. I spent my days writing letters home, getting to know some of my fellow Marines better, and bringing in an occasional resupply chopper.

I reflected on those first 30 days in country. I had survived two major firefights, had taken a small wound to my left shoulder, and had conducted an airstrike and medivac without supervision. I was starting to feel confident, at least in my abilities as a tactical air controlman. I had another village name to add to my growing list of battle areas, Lai An. However, I still had reservations about whether I would be able to survive 13 months of combat duty in the Nam. I looked forward to getting back to the "world," but it was too soon to start counting the days as the short-timers do. I just needed to get through them one day at a time.

CHAPTER

# *EIGHT*

## MILITARY INTELLIGENCE

In the early weeks of June, 1968, we had settled into an easy routine in a small village south of the Song Bo Dieu, a branch of the Cua Viet River just east of Dai Do. It seemed as though we had been removed from the war here, even though I knew we had not. My daily routine had almost become boring. Since we were in a "stand down" mode of operation, there was little need for me as a one four man – no medivac's to handle, no resupply choppers, no aerial observers, or air-strikes. I checked in on my radio periodically with battalion to see if I was needed; but, for the most part, the day was mine to do whatever I pleased as long as I remained in the village.

The village people went about their own routine as though we didn't exist, as though the war didn't exist. There were women and children here. Our presence made them feel safe just as their presence made us feel safe. I'd see the old women working in the rice paddies paying little attention to the Marines nearby.

It was the kids that seemed to be the most intrigued by the Americans. They hung around us, tried to speak some English, and always seemed to have something to sell to us or trade for C-rations. A can of Coca-Cola was the common item for sale, and I never understood how they could come by such a luxury and we couldn't. They would happily sell you a can for a dollar, though, or trade a can for a pack of C-rations.

We didn't really carry money in Vietnam. I was only paid once a month. Usually, I just had my entire pay check sent home to my parents. There wasn't anything you could buy, since we were seldom at a large base where a store even existed. However, I still had a few American dollars in my wallet that I had brought with me from the world.

One little girl kept pestering me to buy some cookies from her. They looked rather plain. I don't know what they were actually made of; I didn't give it much thought. Compared to the sort of things that came in our C-rations, they looked enticing enough. So being a bit soft-hearted and sympathetic, I decided to spend one of my American dollars for a small bag. I saved the cookies for later when I had my C-ration favorite, chicken and noodles.

Had I been in country a bit longer, I probably would not have bought the cookies. I had not yet learned about some of the guerilla warfare that the Viet Cong used against us. After all, my only contact with the enemy had been with the North Vietnamese Army. I hadn't been involved in any engagements with the Viet Cong. I did, however, remember some of my jungle training and that practice ambush by men dressed in the traditional Viet Cong clothing, black pajamas and the cone-shaped straw hats.

That evening I cooked my C-rations and devoured them as usual, being constantly hungry since my arrival in country. I was looking forward to those cookies; but when I took the first bite they were full of ground up glass. I had just learned another lesson of the war, trust no one.

I doubt that the little girl knew the cookies had glass in them. My best guess is that someone gave them to her and told her to sell them to one of the American soldiers. That "someone" was a Viet Cong; and the cookies were intended to harm a U.S. soldier, take him out of the field for a few days, or out of the war. Fortunately, I discovered the glass before I swallowed; no harm had been done.

Those easy-going days in the village also brought another new discovery, Red Cross packages from high school girls back in the world. The packages were simply addressed "To A Marine." Everyone, at one time or another, would get one. This time the cookies were the real thing, and they were simply delicious. My package contained the cookies, some toilet articles such as soap and toothpaste, and a letter from the sender. I eagerly replied to the letter and gained a new pen pal.

It was during this time that I finally received my first letter from home. It took several weeks for our letters to reach home and two or three more weeks to get a reply. Of course I kept in touch with my parents; but it was the letters from my old high school girlfriend, Evelyn, that meant the most to me.

It was difficult to write friends and family, because I never knew exactly what I could or should tell them about the war. There was no way that I could explain the battle of Dai Do or Lai An to my parents. I suspected that just my presence in Vietnam worried them in spite of my mother's mental illnesses. Such descriptive details would have certainly increased their concerns, and I simply had no words at the time to describe those unforgettable events. So I kept my writing simple, for the most part. I talked about the heat, day in and day out, the simple life of these villagers, the lack of any kind of modern conveniences, and the other simple day-to-day routines I was experiencing at the time.

Just the fact that these high school girls were sending us such packages left the impression that the people back in the world cared about us. I'm sure some of these young girls had brothers or even fathers fighting the war, and certainly it was that sort of connection to the war that motivated them to put these packages together and send them. What I didn't know was that angry protests were happening back in the states on a daily basis. I didn't know or realize just how controversial the war had become. (This information was wisely kept from us.)

Like all good things, our easy days soon came to an end; we had received orders for a new operation. We were to attack a village several miles to the south, where intelligence reports stated that a battalion-size unit of NVA had dug in. With all the scuttlebutt that was going around, it looked like Alpha Company was going to be in for another major fight. The CO held a meeting with his platoon leaders, artillery and mortar FO's, and me, the one four man, to discuss the operation. I would probably be needed to handle air support in every form, including the helicopter lift of the company.

A helo lift was a new experience for me, and I was apprehensive. I would be on the first chopper, so I could coordinate tactical air support on the ground at our objective. That meant bringing in the other choppers, running an aerial observer, and possible fixed-wing support if we did engage the NVA in a "hot LZ."

Hot LZ meant that immediately upon landing, the helicopter would come under enemy fire. That scared the hell out of me. Not only had I never ridden in a helicopter, but also this would be my first mission into a suspected enemy position where there was a high probability that the LZ would be hot. I didn't know what to expect and talking with some of the more seasoned vets only made matters worse.

I had heard stories of choppers being shot down, heavy casualties, the chaos and confusion in those early moments of landing; and, then, I recalled the two choppers that I had seen shot down in Dai Do. Thoughts of how I was going to survive this one got the adrenaline flowing again.

At dawn the next day, we packed up our gear and moved to an open rice paddy to await the arrival of the choppers. Bravo one four would control the arriving choppers that would first pick up Alpha Company and lift us to the objective, another rice paddy outside the suspected NVA held village. I would have 17 men with me, on the first chopper, all armed with M-16's, hand grenades, and one M-60 machine gun. To lighten my load, I had managed to ditch my M-16 in exchange for a 45 caliber pistol, so I no longer carried two bandoliers of ammunition. After all, my weapon was my radio.

The 45 pistol was a close range weapon with an effective range of only 50 meters or less. It held only 9 rounds in its clip. I just hoped that I wouldn't have to use it. If I did, that meant the enemy would be right on top of us; and I'd probably be so scared I'd never even get a round off.

As the choppers circled overhead, Bravo one four popped a green smoke grenade in the middle of the paddy to signal where they were to set down. One by one the CH-46's landed in the paddy, about 50 meters in front of us. I checked my weapon and ammunition; I had two clips, 18 rounds in all. I chambered a round but left the safety on; I didn't want to risk having the weapon accidently discharge while we were inside the chopper.

I was also talking with an aerial observer as we prepared to board the choppers. The AO was at the target village directing an artillery strike from eight inch naval guns out in the Gulf of Tonkin. I assumed he was prepping the LZ before we landed.

The engines revved up, and the chopper lifted off. This was my first time inside a CH-46. There were fold-down, fabric-covered seats for us to sit on. There was a tremendous amount of noise inside the chopper. The noise made me feel uncomfortable, because I had learned that hearing certain warning sounds could mean the difference between life and death. Other than the noise of the engines, I could hear nothing.

The flight lasted 10 to 15 minutes. We began a descent, and it felt like a roller coaster going downhill rapidly. It gave me that feeling of my stomach leaping into my throat. The chopper slowed its decent as it leveled out and hovered for a few seconds. Then, it shook a little as it settled on the ground and the tailgate opened.

We all rushed out the back. I was eager to get back onto solid ground. As we exited the aircraft into a dry rice paddy, I suddenly heard automatic weapons fire, machine guns. The adrenaline rushed through my body once more. This could only mean one thing – the LZ was hot.

With the noise of the helicopter and the automatic weapons fire, it was difficult to tell what was going on. Dirt and debris was being blown everywhere. I dropped to the ground. The other Marines had dispersed forming a perimeter around the LZ, facing outwards, waiting for an attack. The chopper lifted off, and the others landed one by one around the general area of the first.

As the noise subsided, I realized that the LZ wasn't hot after all. The automatic weapons fire I had heard actually came from the machine guns on the chopper. Each chopper had two waist gunners who would fire M-60 machine guns outward at the perimeter around the chopper, just in case the chopper came under a ground attack. This was standard operating procedure and another one of those things to add to my growing list of what they didn't teach me in all of that training I had gone through. I guess I'd better add the helo lift to that list as well!

There wasn't much for me to do as far as the air lift was concerned. The choppers all knew where to land; and as each one delivered its troops, the perimeter around me grew, as everyone moved outward. The remainder of the company CP landed, and I joined up with the CO and other members. It wasn't until after the last chopper landed that I realized where the AO was directing that naval gunfire. He wasn't prepping the LZ; he was prepping the village we were about to enter. That made sense. I wondered if an airstrike would be needed.

This village was quite different from the others I had seen. A heavy treeline lay about a thousand meters in front of us, to the southeast; and the village was inside this wooded area. I couldn't see the rounds impacting because of the trees, but I could hear them.

We all knelt down in a crouched position and waited for the artillery barrage to end. There didn't seem to be any sign of activity in the village. That was expected. In my limited experience, the civilian population would leave whenever the NVA came.

When the naval guns stopped firing, the AO radioed to tell me that he had halted the barrage. We could begin to make our assault on the village. I notified the CO who, in turn, radioed one of his platoon leaders and gave the go ahead for the platoon to move forward.

The platoon formed up and began to move across the open rice paddy in single file. The point man approached the treeline. The tension grew as we all anticipated an ambush to be sprung at any minute. I was sure glad that I wasn't among those lead elements. The CO was smart to send a platoon ahead of the rest of the company. If it was an ambush, only a few men would be attacked instead of the entire company.

A gentle breeze could be felt against the sweat dripping from my face; and, for an instant, the coolness gave me a sense of relief and calm. I pulled a canteen from my belt and took a swig of the hot liquid – not nearly as refreshing as the breeze was.

Suddenly, without warning, an explosion at the treeline; I nearly dropped my canteen and was shaken back to reality.

"Booby trap!" the CO's radio operator yelled, as he received word over the radio from the point platoon.

It was the typical booby trap I had been taught about in jungle training. An American hand grenade had been slipped inside an American C-ration can. Apparently, the can had been fastened to the side of a tree; and a trip wire led across a trail that entered the village. The point man had not seen the wire and tripped the booby trap. The irony of it all was that he had been wounded by an American grenade. The NVA were clever to collect our own weapons and use them against us whenever they were given a chance.

The platoon took their wounded man and quickly withdrew, moving back to join the rest of the company. By now Bravo Company was landing in the paddy just north of our position. I radioed the choppers and told them that we had wounded that needed to be medivaced. The company corpsman tended to the man who had taken shrapnel in his legs, and then had a couple of grunts carry him to a nearby chopper, using a makeshift stretcher made from a poncho.

The skipper (CO) wasn't taking any more chances on losing more men. He ordered more naval gunfire on the village. I radioed the AO and gave him the word. Meanwhile, our artillery FO called in an artillery strike of his own. Within minutes, dozens of rounds were impacting inside the treeline.

We must have bombarded that village for another 30 minutes, before the CO halted the barrage and ordered his platoon to move forward again. They approached more cautiously this time, checking diligently for booby traps as well as enemy bunkers.

Moving into the treeline, the platoon disappeared from sight. I could feel the tension growing as we all waited for word from the lead platoon.

The village was secure! It was safe for the company to join up with them inside the village. Bravo Company remained in the rice paddy awaiting further orders.

The booby trap had been set by VC (Viet Cong), **but the NVA were not in this village**. The village was occupied by South Vietnamese – men, women, children, the people we were fighting for.

The awesome American firepower had wreaked havoc on this simple village – **the wrong village**. Many of the villagers had been wounded; some had been killed.

The company corpsmen did what they could to treat the wounded. I still remember the vivid scene of a corpsman trying to treat an old man who had taken a piece of shrapnel to his jaw. Women were crying, huts had been destroyed, lives had been changed – so much for "military intelligence."

As we completed our search of the devastated village, word came over the radio that we were to be helo-lifted to another village several miles north of the Cua Viet River along the coast of the Gulf of Tonkin – the right village. This is where the NVA were, and another Marine company was in heavy contact and needed us for backup.

We quickly assembled in teams of 18 outside the village in the same rice paddy where we had landed. I marked the LZ with a smoke grenade now knowing that it was safe here. This time I would go out on the last chopper, so I could control the airlift while the company one four man in the other company controlled the landing. The corpsmen brought some of the village wounded to the LZ to be evacuated to Quang Tri for treatment.

When I finally landed at the new village LZ, I could hear small arms fire to my north. Alpha and Bravo companies had formed a protective perimeter. Then, the waiting began.

There were bomb craters and artillery craters all around us. I took up a position near an artillery crater, which I knew would provide me with some protection should we begin to take incoming. No sooner had that thought entered my mind than the familiar "pop" of NVA artillery could be heard far off to the north. Before I could get the words out of my mouth, someone shouted, "Incoming!"

I dived for the crater and curled up into a fetal position trying to make myself as small a target as possible. The screaming of the incoming round raced over my head, impacting far to the south of our position. Perhaps we weren't the target, or the NVA gunners were just bad shots.

More rounds were fired. Each time they impacted, they came closer to our position. I was later told that often the NVA would walk the rounds backwards from the first impact, so they covered a larger area and improved the chances they would hit something. It was a common practice even for our own artillery.

We stayed in our current position for the remainder of the day. I dug a foxhole, since it didn't look like we were going anywhere soon. Airstrikes were called in by the one four man of the company engaged with the NVA. Trying to learn anything new that might help me in the future, I listened to the radio traffic between him and an aerial observer.

As night descended upon us, I broke out my C-rations and heated up a can of ham slices using a small chunk of C-4 explosives. (C-4 is a plastic explosive that was used by engineers to blow up bunkers or clear trees for an LZ. It had become common practice to use it also to heat C-rations. A small chunk about one half inch square would burn intensely and boil water in seconds. Using any larger piece, you could easily melt the can itself. It wouldn't explode if you lit it with a match; that required a blasting cap.)

We didn't take any more incoming that night, but the company we had been sent to support continued to fight sporadically. When morning arrived, we received new orders once again. Now we were being lifted to another area to the west. Another company of Marines on a mountaintop had been attacked during the night, and we were going there to reinforce them. These constant changes and movements reminded me of something the grunts joked about frequently – the Nam was nothing but a three-ring circus; everyone ran around in circles, but no one seemed to know what was going on. The grunts would whistle the organ music associated with a circus.

We repeated the routine of loading our gear and boarding choppers to take us to the mountains. I was a bit concerned that we might come under another artillery barrage from the north, but none came. I boarded a chopper, and we lifted off heading west.

As I looked out the small window at the landscape below, we moved away from the flatlands, and the terrain changed to hills and mountains. We passed over one area where I could see craters below. It looked like the face of the moon; craters from a B-52 strike peppered an area several miles long. I was told that a B-52 strike usually consisted of 6 bombers each carrying over a hundred 500 pound bombs. They would blanket a large area where there was a suspected enemy complex or infiltration route. There were no villages in this area. It was a "free fire zone" – anything was a target and anyone was the enemy.

The chopper pulled into a circular pattern banking to the left as it approached a barren hilltop. As I peered out the window at the ground below, I saw a new sight, a fire support base nestled atop a mountain.

The northern I Corps area had been trying a new strategy, moving artillery batteries out into the mountains so they could support ground troops moving deeper into the enemy's territory. Ground troops would first be lifted onto a mountain to secure the area. Engineers would be brought by chopper along with bulldozers to clear the hill and dig gun pits. Once the pits had been prepared, the artillery guns would be brought in, also by chopper. It was a new concept, and I Corps Marines were pushing deeper than ever into enemy territory with full artillery and air support.

The chopper descended upon one end of the mountaintop, pulled into a hover, and then settled its back wheels on the ground. The tailgate came down, and we quickly exited. We were atop the very peak of a large, barren mountain surrounded by a dense jungle. Six 105 millimeter howitzers were strung out in a line across a ridge which jutted out from the peak of the mountain. Each howitzer was set up in a crater that had been dug out by the engineers.

*CH-46 Landing on Mountaintop*

I learned that the fire support base (FSB) had been attacked during the night by a large enemy unit. I saw barbed wire strung around the perimeter of the hill and several NVA bodies caught in the wire. The sight of dead bodies had become routine now. I took it all in stride, not really giving it so much as a second thought. Better them than me, I figured – one less gook I've got to worry about trying to kill me.

Typically the FSB would consist of an artillery battery of 6 guns and approximately 8 men per gun. The battery would be protected by a company of Marines, approximately 150 men.

*Fire Support Base on Mountaintop*

*105 millimeter Howitzer on FSB*

Alpha Company had been sent in to provide additional support in case of another attack. The FSB was atop a mountain near Khe Sanh, which had been the scene of a major NVA attack earlier during the Tet Offensive of 1968. There was still a concentration of NVA troops in the areas around Khe Sanh.

As another day in the Nam came to an end, I dug my foxhole as far away from the big guns as I could get while still being inside our own perimeter. If I had learned anything in my short term here, it was to stay away from any obvious target for incoming.

The events of the day were still nagging me. How could that attack on a friendly village happen? What if I had been ordered to direct an airstrike on that village? I could have killed dozens of innocent people. It is one thing to fire on a village when someone inside is firing at you; but to begin firing without any provocation from the village is something else. Military intelligence is not always correct. Attacking that village was "one for the lesson book" – don't direct an airstrike on a village if you are not engaged in actual fighting. I did not want to have to live out the rest of my life knowing that I might have killed dozens of innocent people.

CHAPTER

# *NINE*

## BACK TO LAI AN

As June came to an end, we were once again helo-lifted back to the flat lands to another village on the north side of the Cua Viet River. There were rumors floating around that we would soon be going back to the village of Lai An, where I had been wounded a few months earlier. Days before the operation kicked off, I could hear B-52 "arc lights" to the north along the DMZ. Recalling our previous operation in that area, those missions gave me a sense of security, knowing that such heavy concentrations of bombing would have a positive effect on eliminating the threat of NVA artillery support.

On the eve of our departure, I learned from a briefing with the company CP that this operation would involve the entire regiment – 1st, 2nd and 3rd Battalions. Our mission was to eliminate the NVA infiltration that had been going on since

April. This regimental sweep would possibly take us inside the DMZ. Our battalion would pass through Lai An and push to the DMZ while the other battalions would expand the mission to the east and west of us. This would result in a complete "search and destroy" effort from the coast to Highway 1, which ran north/south from Dong Ha to North Vietnam. We could expect heavy enemy contact, and tanks would accompany us to help route the NVA from suspected bunker complexes across the entire area.

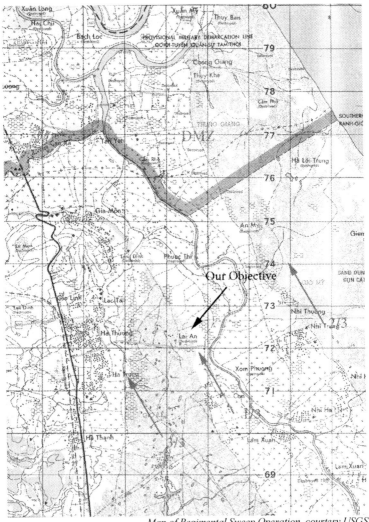

*Map of Regimental Sweep Operation, courtesy USGS*

For the remainder of the day, I wrote some letters trying to take my mind off of the impending operation; but I couldn't stop thinking about the possibility of a major battle looming ahead. Approximately 1000 leathernecks would be involved in this operation, making this the largest one yet in which I would participate. In an operation of this magnitude, I would surely be called upon to control every kind of air support available.

That night I found it difficult to sleep. I could hear the continued B-52 strikes to the north and knew that this could be the battle that would kill me. Even though the battles I had already experienced (Dai Do and first Lai An) were intense, such concentrated preparatory bombing was not used in either battle. This could only mean one thing – tomorrow's mission would probably be the mother of battles in comparison.

At first light, we packed up our gear and began the march back north. Everyone was loaded up with lots of ammunition; I was becoming accustomed to the weight of my load. Without the M-16, I was actually carrying less than I had the first time we fought in Lai An.

Our battalion was spread out in several long columns, each consisting of a company of men. Battalion headquarters was in the middle column, our company at the rear. Alpha company would take point when we approached our objective. It brought back the memories I had of my grandmother's words, "The Marines are the first to fight, Bobby." First to fight, that would surely be the case this day. If the NVA were there, the point company, my company, would be the first to engage them.

We were following a small river that was actually a branch of the Ben Hai River in the DMZ. Our trek northward took us past numerous villages. South Vietnamese peasants worked the rice fields we walked through. They ignored the leathernecks passing by, which made me wonder if they knew something we didn't know.

When we were a few thousand meters from Lai An, the other companies began to spread out to our east and west, while Alpha company remained focused on the village. To our east was $2^{nd}$ Battalion, and to our west was $3^{rd}$ Battalion – a wide line of fighting Marines.

The map indicated that we were approaching a road that connected the river to the east with Highway 1 to the west. Lai An lay just beyond the road in the sand dunes.

Our point platoon approached the road as the company CP began to cross a large rice paddy. I stopped for a moment to take a drink of water and wipe the sweat dripping from my brow. It would be dark soon. We should be stopping our advance, so that we could dig in for the night.

Crack! Crack! Crack! Alpha Company had just made contact with the enemy; the point platoon had walked into an ambush.

We quickly spread out, and the CO moved forward. I hit the ground and waited to see what would happen, but it was only for a moment.

"One four man up!" the CO yelled.

That's my call – I jumped to my feet and dashed forward. The CO, artillery FO, and 81 mortar FO had taken a position behind a hedgerow just south of the road. The battle quickly intensified several hundred meters in front of us.

I wondered where those tanks were; they were supposed to be providing support. Apparently, they were supporting one of the other battalions, although we were the ones to make contact.

"Hunt, I need some air support over the village. It's going to get dark soon, and I need to know what we're up against."

"Roger that, skipper. Candy Tuff one four, this is Alpha one four, over."

"Alpha one four, Candy Tuff one four, over."

"Candy Tuff, this is Alpha. Request AO, grid two four seven two, over."

"Roger, Alpha one four, out."

I waited impatiently for an AO to arrive. The sun would be setting soon, and we really needed to have some idea of the size of the force in front of us. We weren't taking incoming, but that didn't make the wait any easier.

"Alpha one four, this is Badger seven, over."

"Aahh roger, Badger seven, Alpha one four. I need you to check out grid square two four seven two. We're in contact, need to know what we're up against, over."

"Alpha, we're a pair of gunships. We'll see what we can do for you."

Huey Gunships – I was expecting an O-1 Bird Dog.

"Alpha, this is Badger. I'm not sure we can be of much help. I can't see much on the ground in this kind of light, over."

"Wait one, Badger," I replied. Darkness was quickly approaching by the time the Hueys had reached our area. The pilot couldn't see the target grid. I explained the situation to the CO.

The 81 mortar FO had an idea. By now the mortar crew had set up and was ready for a fire mission. The FO suggested he run an illumination mission. The mortars could fire a special round that would explode over the target deploying a flare on a parachute. This would light up the target and enable the Huey's to see. As far as I knew, this had never been tried before.

"Badger seven, this is Alpha one four. We're going to fire an illum round over the target area. Let me know if that helps, over."

"Aahh roger, Alpha. What's your position, Alpha?"

"I'm at your two o'clock. Turning on strobe light, over."

Gordon had given me his strobe light just before leaving Vietnam. The light was to be used in darkness to show aircraft your position. You would place your helmet on the ground, open side up, and place the strobe inside. The strobe would turn on and off in a rhythmic fashion and could be seen only from the air.

"Roger, I have your pos. What's the run-in, over?"

"Zero two zero, over."

"Roger that, Alpha."

Within five minutes, the illumination mortar was on its way. The pilots had turned on their flashing red lights, and I could see and hear them to the west of me.

"Rounds out, Badger," I radioed the pilot.

"Roger, rounds out."

There was a faint pop as the illumination round exploded high over the village of Lai An; the sky lit up as its parachute deployed.

"Alpha one four, this is Badger seven. Your illum is right on target. I can see the vill. Where are your people, Alpha?"

"Skipper, where is the lead platoon?" I asked the CO.

"They've moved back to the road and are digging in along its south edge."

"Badger, this is Alpha. Just north of my position about two hundred meters, over."

"Aahh roger. It looks like we might have an enemy machine gun position in sight. I see some mounds that might be bunkers. Don't see any troops. I'm firing a Willie Pete at that machine gun position. Let me know how that looks, over."

The Huey fired a rocket, and a plume of yellow lit up the chopper as it whisked away. Seconds later, it impacted in a ball of white fire, and large, white sparks emanated outward in a full 360 degree circle for 50 yards or more. I'd never seen white phosphorous explode at night.

The CO called his forward platoon on the radio to make sure that the target was an adequate distance from them.

"We're good, Hunt. Let 'er rip!" the CO shouted.

"Roger, Badger. We're good, over."

"Let us swing around again, Alpha. Tell me when you're ready to light 'er up, over."

The choppers peeled off to the west and circled back so that they could get set up on the run-in heading again. I stood next to the mortar FO, and he called for all six tubes to light up the target area.

"Rounds out, Badger."

The sky exploded with light as six illumination rounds floated gently to earth on their small parachutes. Moments later the first Huey let loose with a dozen rockets with machine guns blazing. Six strings of red tracer bullets could be seen flying towards the target (every fifth round of the machine guns bullets were tracers). It was the most awesome airstrike I had ever seen. It reminded me of the Fourth of July. And then it dawned on me, it actually was July 4th!

This scene was repeated several times, until the Hueys had exhausted all of their ammunition.

"Alpha, this is Badger, we're out of ammo, but we'll head back and reload. This was so much fun, we want to do it again, over!"

Unfortunately, we had expended all of our 81 mortar illumination rounds and could not run the mission again. The Hueys returned to their base as I began digging my foxhole in the dark. This first day of the battle had been more fun than fear – a welcome relief from previous battles. We hadn't suffered any casualties, and I had gained some great experience. I felt good about myself; I was becoming a seasoned vet. Now, all I had to do was to survive the remaining ten months!

The next morning, we continued our advance northward. It wasn't long before I heard the tubes pop; incoming artillery began to pound our position and halted our advance.

Pop! Pop! Pop! Round after round began exploding within our lines. The terrain was sandy and there were no foxholes, only craters from our previous battle here. I crawled into a shallow crater and curled up into a ball. This was the worst artillery barrage I had experienced – 130 millimeter artillery rounds, 85 millimeter artillery rounds, and 61 and 82 millimeter mortars were exploding everywhere. I could hear the shrapnel piercing the air all around me. I couldn't move; none of us could. Rounds impacted so close at times that they kicked sand into my shallow crater.

I called battalion and requested an aerial observer, in hopes that he could fly northward and locate the guns that were firing at us.

"Alpha one four, this is Jawbreaker Tango, over."

The AO had arrived on station. I briefed him on our predicament. He headed north, far to our east, near the coast to stay out of the line of fire.

Thankfully, that familiar call for me to move up never came, and I was able to remain in my crater during this intense bombardment. The incoming lasted for over an hour. I later learned that we had taken over 50 rounds of 130 millimeter artillery during that time, an almost unprecedented amount when you consider the tons of bombs our B-52's had dropped on North Vietnam days before our arrival. The bombing had done nothing to deter the pounding we took that day. Fortunately we suffered very few casualties.

The AO had spotted some guns deep inside North Vietnam and called for a strike of 2000 pound rounds from the U.S.S. New Jersey, which was sitting off the coast in the Gulf of

Tonkin. The New Jersey fired shells that were 16 inches in diameter and weighed as much as a small car. I had been told that, when the ship fired all of its guns, it would physically move 6 inches sideways in the water. Also when one of its rounds exploded, anything within a 1000 meter radius would be destroyed. It was the most powerful weapon in use in Vietnam.

When the shelling finally stopped, I crawled out of my hole and located the CO who was just a few short meters away in his own small crater. The company went on the attack again, pushing through Lai An village.

The tanks had now joined us and moved to the front to destroy enemy bunkers. They encountered heavy resistance, taking heavy weapons fire such as RPG rockets and 60 millimeter mortars. Our infantry was right behind them, providing their own counterfire. It must have looked like something straight out of a John Wayne movie, as the leathernecks fought hard to take the same terrain we had taken a few months earlier. The NVA were determined; they did not want to give up this piece of real estate.

As the battle reached its peak, the CO, his radio operator, and I moved forward within a hundred meters of our front lines. We jumped into a bomb crater just when I heard more pops of incoming artillery. Seconds later, the artillery began falling all around us again.

This time the order was to keep pushing northward. We weren't waiting like sitting ducks for a possible counter attack. Often the NVA would use this strategy. They would fire artillery in front of them to get the Marines to take cover and keep their heads down, not watching what was going on in front of them. During that time, the NVA would launch a counterattack and shut down the artillery barrage just as they charged the Marines, quickly overrunning their position.

We were running forward, 20 or 30 meters at a time before diving into the nearest bomb crater or hole, as the enemy continued to pound us with their artillery. Our company was charging the enemy position, determined to route them once and for all. The shells were exploding all around us. Our tanks were firing point blank range at NVA bunkers. It seemed like total chaos, with all the explosions and small arms fire coming from both us and the NVA. As we continued to push forward however, I knew that we were gaining the upper hand.

We dove into another bomb crater to take cover from the incoming artillery. There were a few grunts in the crater; and outside, tied up with rope, was an NVA prisoner the grunts had captured. The prisoner was alive, blindfolded with his hands tied behind his back. I thought it was ironic that he lay outside the crater exposed to his own exploding weapons; he would probably be killed by his own people.

The midday heat was taking its toll on me. We had been fighting all morning, and I had used up all my water. The sun was relentless. Often the temperature would reach 130 degrees at this time of day. With the constant fighting, constant incoming, and continuous push forward, there had been no time to bring in any resupplies or even run an airstrike. The AO was staying to the east of us along the coast, because the incoming posed a serious problem for him, too.

My thirst was becoming insatiable – I needed water. I didn't want to ask someone else for a drink, because they were in the same situation as I and needed it as badly. At the bottom of the bomb crater was a pool of water. It was as black as coffee. I contemplated drinking the murky water for only a few seconds. Had it been a different situation I would not have given it a thought, but war changes the equation; you forget about cleanliness and sanitation, and throw all such inhibitions out the window. I crawled to the bottom of the crater, took out a canteen, and filled it. Then, I dropped two halazone tablets the corpsman had given me for just such a situation. After briefly closing the lid and shaking the contents to dissolve the tablets, I took a drink. The taste was pungent, but it was wet. I returned to the top edge of the crater and passed the canteen around. The others were appreciative of the gesture.

The combination of tanks and Marine infantry finally proved successful, and our company defeated the entrenched NVA soldiers. Over the next several days, we moved farther northward to within a few hundred meters of the DMZ. This was about as close as you could get to North Vietnam.

Sporadic fighting continued each day. I ran a few air-strikes on bunker positions. We took more incoming, and our artillery and mortar FO's stayed busy running their own missions. Alpha Company casualties were light considering the intensity of the battle – 12 wounded and one killed. The wounded were sent south to one of our other companies who handled the medivac's. We had persevered; we had won another decisive battle in Lai An. I hoped this would be our last one here.

On the evening of July 8<sup>th</sup>, I was talking with an aerial observer who was checking out an area north of the Ben Hai River.

"Alpha one four, this is Jawbreaker. Do you have any men north of the river?" the AO asked.

"Say again, Jawbreaker!" I replied. Was I hearing him correctly?

"I say again, do you have men north of the river, over?"

"Not that I know of. I don't think we're allowed to go north of the river; but I'll check. Wait one, out," I replied.

I quickly found the skipper and asked him if we had any men north of the river. He didn't think so but radioed battalion to ask the question. The response was as expected, a resounding "no!"

"Jawbreaker Tango, this is Alpha one four. That's a negative, over."

"Roger that, Alpha. Well, I've got a hundred troops or more, in the open, headed your way. I'm calling in naval gunfire. Tell your six, over."

"Oh boy, here we go again," I muttered to myself. I told the skipper. He, in turn, relayed the message to battalion who then relayed it to regimental command. Fifteen minutes later we received new orders – pack up, we're heading back to the Cua Viet River! A new operation was being planned, and we would be heading out for somewhere else in a day or two.

I couldn't believe it! After fighting for several days and for the second time in two months, with more NVA now headed our way, we were being pulled out of the area and giving it back to the enemy. This was insane, I thought to myself. Had this kind of strategy been used in World War II, I had no doubt we would have lost that war. I could not understand why we would do such a thing. Just what had we accomplished? We had fought gallantly for this worthless piece of real estate, twice – a lousy village of straw and sticks. And now we were just going to leave and give it all back, and for what?

Now, as I reflect on that event, I think the situation was as frustrating for my commanders as it was for me. There simply weren't enough troops in this area to handle the heavy infiltration from the north. It was like trying to plug holes in the proverbial dike – you'd plug up one hole only to have another spring a leak somewhere else.

I packed up and assembled with the CP as quickly as I could. First Platoon was already moving out, taking the point on another eight mile trek back to the Cua Viet River. We'd get no sleep tonight. I could hear the naval gunfire impacting to the north. I radioed the aerial observer and let him know that we were departing the area. He seemed as surprised as I about the news.

The battle of Lai An, from July 4 through July 8, 1968, had earned 1st Battalion, 3rd Marine Regiment, a Meritorious Unit

Commendation. The following is a copy of that commendation:

—*—— —*—— —*—— —*—— —*—— —*—— —*—— —*—— —*—— —*—

*"The Secretary of the Navy takes pleasure in presenting the MERITORIOUS UNIT COMMENDATION to*

*FIRST BATTALION, THIRD MARINES (REINFORCED) THIRD MARINE DIVISION (REINFORCED) FLEET MARINE FORCE*

*For service as set forth in the following*

*CITATION:*

*For meritorious service in connection with operations against North Vietnamese Army forces in the Republic of Vietnam from 4 to 8 July 1968. On 4 July the First Battalion, Third Marines (Reinforced) moved north from Mai Xa Thi for Lai An. Late in the afternoon, along the southern limits of Lai An, the leading company made initial contact with a North Vietnamese Army unit estimated to be approximately 20 North Vietnamese soldiers. As the battle developed, the enemy force began to disclose itself and increased in size to approximately 100 men with semiautomatic and automatic weapons in a well constructed, mutually supporting bunker complex supported by 60 mm and 82 mm mortars and 85 mm and 130 mm artillery. Contact with the North Vietnamese Army unit was maintained throughout the night. Early on the next morning the attack continued. Maximum use was made of all supporting arms, tanks, artillery, naval gunfire, and air to dislodge the stubborn defenders. In spite of heavy pounding of enemy positions by supporting arms, the enemy continued to courageously defend his position and had to be routed or killed in place by continuous tank-infantry coordinated attack. As attacking forces slowly moved forward, the enemy intensified his defensive fires to include skillful use of his own supporting arms. The battalion came under frequent periods of intense mortar and artillery fire. Throughout the*

*5th, 6th and 7th of July, the advance slowly continued. The operation was successful because of the close-in infantry attacks, well coordinated with the skillful use of supporting arms, inflicting on the enemy heavy losses of personnel, ammunition, and supplies. Through the courageous determination, indomitable spirit, intrepidity, and extraordinary professionalism, the officers and men of the First Battalion, Third Marines (Reinforced) upheld the highest traditions of the Marine Corps and the United States Naval Service.*

*For the Secretary of the Navy,*

*Commandant of the Marine Corps"*

# CHAPTER

# *TEN*

## MUTTER'S RIDGE

When we returned to the Cua Viet River from our operation in Lai An, our tactical area of responsibility (TAOR) was changed. We were moved from the flatlands of rice paddies and small villages to the mountains of jungles and rain forests. I couldn't help wondering what type of action I might see in this new area. I had been in country less than three months now, and already I had seen three major battles. I had been wounded, and our battalion had earned two unit commendations. This was shaping up to be one hell of a tour of duty.

We marched out to Route 1 where we were loaded onto trucks. The convoy took us down Route 9 which extends westward and southward as far as Khe Sanh. We passed the last large village before the mountains – Cam Lo, the outpost

A-3, and the larger base, Camp Carroll. Our final destination was a small base called "The Rockpile."

The Rockpile got its name from a large mountain of solid rock that stood a few thousand meters to the south of the Marine base. Northwest of the mountain was a larger rock mountain called "The Razorback." The base sat on a small, barren hill between these two major land features.

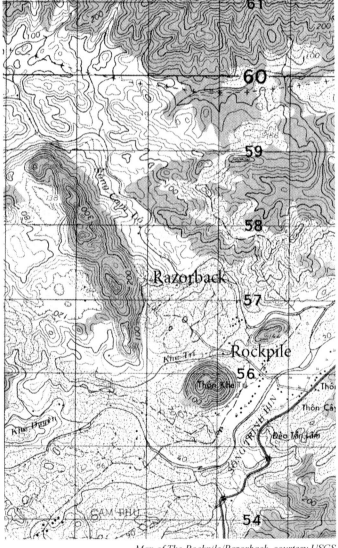

*Map of The Rockpile/Razorback, courtesy USGS*

Several miles to the south of the Rockpile was another, much larger base called Vandegrift Airbase, better known as LZ Studd. This new base was to replace Khe Sanh, which had been closed and abandoned after the January Tet Offensive. LZ Studd had a runway that could accommodate C-130 transport planes as well as many helicopters. It would be used to launch operations to the west and south while the Rockpile and Camp Carroll would be used to launch operations to the west and north. The Rockpile also had an artillery unit which could fire in support of units operating in this mountainous region.

Alpha Company was given temporary duty as perimeter guard at the Rockpile. The other companies of the battalion were given similar duty at other small outposts.

To myself, I questioned why we were pulled out of Lai An so quickly, if all we were going to do was stand perimeter guard here. There had to be something much larger developing.

The first thing I observed about the Rockpile was that most of the base was underground. This could only mean one thing, frequent incoming. We were still fairly close to the DMZ; and the terrain to the north and west of the base was nothing but mountains, a type of terrain that provided the enemy with excellent cover and protection from aerial detection because of the triple canopy of the jungle. Enemy guns could be easily concealed, but the terrain also made it very difficult for them to move heavy equipment into the area. The enemy did not have helicopters to move equipment as we did. Instead, they had to move everything on the ground. This meant building roads, usually by hand, and in such a manner that the roads could not be seen from above.

The base consisted of sand-bagged bunkers both above and below ground level. Both had certain advantages and disadvantages. While the bunkers below ground provided better protection from incoming, they also provided better homes for rats, a common problem for any unit that spent time here. Regardless, I wasn't taking any chances and set up my temporary home in one of the underground bunkers. The good news was that the bunkers had cots, which meant a better night's sleep.

There was an 81 millimeter mortar position on the base as well. Having the mortars close by for support was a good thing, but these guns also made good targets and invited enemy fire.

On top of the Razorback was a small outpost used for observation of enemy movement. This position was easy to defend due to its sheer rock cliffs, and its small footprint on top of this steep mountain made it virtually impossible to hit with artillery or mortars. Usually only a squad of men would defend this position, and they had to be lifted in by helicopter.

*The Rockpile Base*

Since convoys of trucks traveled routinely from Dong Ha to the Rockpile and LZ Studd, Route 9 had to be swept for mines every day. Often, I was required to go on the mine sweeping patrol just in case air support was needed. The patrol consisted of a platoon of grunts and one tank. I rode on top of the tank, while two men with metal detectors walked in front sweeping for mines in the road. The grunts walked on each side in a long column to provide protection if the NVA or Viet Cong launched a ground attack. Fortunately, we never were attacked and never found any mines.

*Mine sweeping patrol*

It was at the Rockpile that I met Terry. Terry was a new radio operator who had just arrived in country as replacement for the CO's radio operator who had finished his tour and rotated back to the world. For some reason, Terry and I hit it off right from the start. We were about the same age, same height and weight, and we had much in common.

Terry was from Los Angeles and had gone through the same radio/telegraph school as I. He had been in college but decided that it wasn't what he wanted to do and volunteered for the Marines, just as I had. Because he was from

California, he was familiar with some of the places I had frequented when I was stationed in San Diego. All of these things gave us much to talk about.

Terry wanted to know everything I had learned about Vietnam. We would spend hours just talking. I told him about the battles I had already participated in, about my job as the company one four man, how I had been wounded, and about the heavy artillery barrages we had encountered near the DMZ.

In turn, I wanted to know what was going on back in the world. What was I missing. We talked about the music and who our favorite rock group was. We talked about girls, our favorite foods, and experiences we could brag about or laugh about, such as my broken jaw. Most importantly, we'd talk about what we were going to do when we left this place and were back in the real world. In the short time I spent at the Rockpile, Terry and I became good friends. It was a good feeling to have a friend, someone you could relate to, someone you could talk to and share experiences with, someone you could confide in. Since my arrival in country, this was something that had been lacking for me. Having a friend introduced a bit of normalcy and, somehow, gave me hope that I just might make it out of here alive.

We weren't at the Rockpile for long before the rumors trickled down that 1/3 would soon be going to a mountainous area to the north called Mutter's Ridge. Because Terry was the CO's radio operator, he often was privy to such information by way of radio conversations between the CO and battalion. The scuttlebutt gave us more to talk about, and we sought out more information about Mutter's Ridge from the grunts.

Mutter's Ridge was a ridgeline of mountains that extended east/west from Cam Lo village to the border with Laos, parallel to the DMZ. The last time Marine's had occupied this ridgeline was in 1966. They had assaulted the ridge to seize and take control of hills 400 and 484 in a battle called

Nui Cay Tre Ridge. The call sign of the Marine units in this battle was "Mutter," and when the Marines finally took the hills, they renamed it "Mutter's Ridge" in their own honor. No one had occupied the ridge since then.

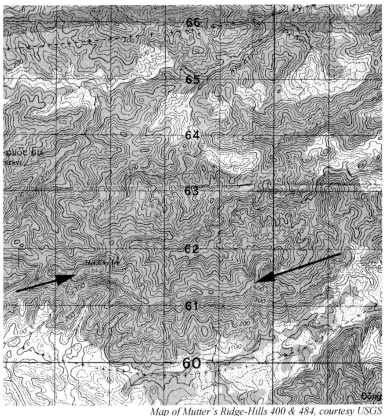

*Map of Mutter's Ridge-Hills 400 & 484, courtesy USGS*

I was sitting in my bunker one day when Terry entered.

"Hey man, wanna go to chow? " Terry asked.

"Might as well, can't dance! " I replied.

"Yeah, and it's too wet to plow! " Terry replied.

"Ain't no babies to kill, no villages to burn. " I said.

This exchange had become a sort of joke among the Marines whenever someone asked you if you wanted to do something. People back in the world were turning against our military and its involvement in the war. News reports were painting a dim picture of how the war was going. The perception of the American people was that the typical combat soldier was a baby killer who burned down villages.

"Ya think we'll see much action?" Terry asked.

"I think so, Terry. I mean, they wouldn't be sending us there if they didn't have some good reasons."

"Cool man, can't wait to see some action!" he replied.

"Believe me man, you *do not* want to see *action*. Combat is the pits, man, bad news. You could get killed!"

"Yeah, but we're radio operators, we're not on the front lines, the grunts do the fighting, right?"

"Wrong, man! No place is safe when you're in a firefight. How the hell do you think I got wounded, man? Incoming! Every man's a target when you're in a firefight. This could be some bad shit, man! It scares the hell outa' me! Who knows what we'll encounter there!" I replied.

I had heard rumors that there were dangerous animals such as rock apes, bamboo vipers and tigers in these triple canopy jungles (three distinct layers of vegetation). The heat was even more intense than what we had experienced in the flatlands. It was August, the peak of summer; and the thick vegetation blocked the sun, trapping the humidity and making it feel even hotter than it actually was (up to 130° F factoring in the humidity). We would have many different enemies to worry about in this type of terrain besides the NVA. The odds of survival were beginning to stack up against us with the threat of wild animals, intense heat and humidity, rugged terrain, and the various forms of enemy threats such as artillery, mortars, booby traps, and ambushes. Apprehension grew as we waited for the operation to begin.

Wisely, regiment had decided to give us a taste of what to expect by sending us to a mountain of similar height outside LZ Studd. The area was much safer; and it was less likely that we would encounter the enemy in this area, yet it would provide us with the experience of humping the steep mountain and enduring the relentless heat. We boarded trucks to take us southward to this new training area.

For the next several days, we hiked up and down steep mountains with the same full load of equipment that we would carry to Mutter's Ridge. The mountains had no trails and were littered with rocks and large boulders. The climb was slow and treacherous. Each step had to be taken carefully, or you could easily twist your ankle trying to negotiate an outcrop of rocks and boulders. The point man hacked a trail with a machete as the company followed close behind in one long line. I couldn't imagine what this would be like on Mutter's Ridge, where the possibility of enemy attack complicated the climb even more. This experience would soon prove to be invaluable.

After several days of this mountain climbing exercise, we were ready for the real thing. Our mission was to set up several new landing zones (LZ's) on the top of Mutter's ridge. These LZ's would be used by companies who would launch patrols in the area. To provide additional support, a Fire Support Base (FSB) would also be built by engineers. FSB Mac, as it would be called, could then provide artillery support to Marine infantry operating in this mountainous region.

Due to the nature of the terrain, the only access we would have to resupply would be by helicopter. I would probably be kept very busy controlling the air support; and, if we did make enemy contact, air-strikes would be needed to open holes in the jungle and destroy bunker and tunnel complexes. This area had a history of NVA infiltration.

The company would be helo-lifted to a grassy field at the southern base of hill 400. From there, we would climb to the top of the mountain where the first LZ would be built. Our next objective would be to the west on hill 484 where the FSB would be built. We would continue our westward trek along Mutter's Ridge to hill 461 where another LZ would be built. Our final objective would be on a mountaintop situated less than a thousand meters from the DMZ. The total distance, as the crow flies, from that first mountaintop to the final one was about 5 miles. However, considering the nature of the terrain, we would probably be walking more than 7 miles, through unexplored jungle.

The airlift to our LZ went smoothly, without any incidents. Once the entire company was on the ground, third platoon took the point as we began our ascent up the mountain. The terrain was similar to what we had practiced on a few days earlier.

We hadn't moved more than a few hundred meters up the mountain before the familiar words came down the column – "Corpsman up!" The intense heat had claimed its first casualty.

"One four man up!" I worked my way up the trail passing Marines one by one. The trail was narrow, steep, and difficult to climb. After 20 minutes of climbing and struggling with that 25 pound radio on my back, I reached the company corpsman.

"Hunt, I need a priority medivac, heat stroke."

"Roger that." I radioed regiment this time and requested the medivac chopper. While I waited, I moved around the area looking for a way to land the helicopter. That just wasn't going to happen in this terrain. The hill was too steep, and the jungle was too thick. I found a slight opening in the trees and decided that I would need to have a line dropped down from the chopper to have the man lifted out. This was something new for me and certainly wasn't something Gordon had taught me. Operating in mountainous terrain was much different than operating in the flatlands.

"Alpha one four, this is Ripcord Romeo, inbound. What is your position, over?"

"Ripcord, this is Alpha one four. My coordinates are approximately niner niner seven, six zero five. I'm popping green smoke, over."

It was difficult to tell exactly where we were. I knew the coordinates of our drop zone and could only estimate my current position because the jungle was too dense to see other recognizable terrain features, such as other mountaintops. Since the LZ was cold (no enemy contact) and the jungle was too dense to use a mirror, I felt that my only choice to signal my position was to pop a smoke grenade.

"Roger, Alpha. I have your smoke in sight. Doesn't look like I'm going to be able to land. I'll lower a hoist."

"Roger that, Ripcord."

The chopper would have to hover over my position and lower a steel cable from a special winch that could be swung out from the side. This cable had a padded harness on the end, which could be put around a man's chest allowing the chopper to extract him from the dense jungle.

As the chopper approached, the prop wash from his rotors kicked up a lot of dust and loose debris making it difficult to see; and the noise made it impossible to hear any enemy fire we might take. I felt very vulnerable at this moment but kept focused on what I was doing.

The corpsman and another Marine moved the heat stroke victim to my position as we all prepared for the extraction. In spite of the noise, I had to give voice guidance to the chopper as he lowered the cable close enough to strap the man in.

"Ripcord, this is Alpha one four. You're a go for extraction, over."

"Roger, Alpha."

We had strapped the man to the cable using the harness. Slowly, he rose as the cable was winched upward, his body spiraling through the opening in the trees. Minutes later the chopper crew had the man. Once they pulled him inside, the chopper lifted and turned southward.

I kept my position in the line as third platoon continued its trek up the mountain, thankful that the medivac went off without a hitch and without enemy contact. Apparently, we were in a fairly secure area. Perhaps this operation wouldn't be so bad after all.

We had ascended no more than 100 meters before the words rang out again, "One four man up!" The heat had claimed another casualty. I took out a salt tablet and washed it down with a swig of hot water from my canteen before descending the hill about 200 meters. I had just taken one step forward and two steps back. I would have to traverse the same ground all over again, going down the mountain and then back up again.

The heat and humidity made my muscles feel like rubber. The weight of my equipment and radio only added to the weakness I felt. I had to descend cautiously because the ground had lots of loose rocks. The dense jungle gave me a sort of claustrophobic feeling, like being surrounded on each side by a wall. It was that dense jungle wall that kept any kind of breeze from blowing, amplifying the intensity of the heat.

This routine of ascending and descending the mountain occurred three times that day before I reached the top. I had to wonder who would have controlled the medivac if I had fallen victim to the heat. It was an exhausting day for us. I could not imagine what it might have been like if we had made contact with the enemy.

As I reached the top of the mountain, I took another swig of hot water from my fourth canteen. I was nearly out of water, everyone was. My next task would be to bring in a resupply chopper with food and water. I pondered just how difficult that task was going to be when suddenly I broke out into the open. The top of the mountain was barren. All of the trees had been blown away from bombing prior to our landing. All that was left was a thick layer of dust. What kind of bomb does this, I wondered. There was no crater like those I had seen from bombs dropped in the flatlands.

I later learned about another weapon used for this sort of preparation – the Daisy Cutter. The Daisy Cutter was a special 15,000 pound bomb with a fuse that extended 38" outward. It was dropped by a flying crane helicopter and would explode above the ground without leaving a crater. It was first used in Vietnam to clear mountaintops – instant LZ.

What I couldn't understand was why we had to climb this mountain when the top of it was clear, void of all trees. Helicopters could have easily set down on top rather than make us climb and lose men to the heat. Again, I wondered if the people making these decisions really knew what they were doing. No wonder the grunts equated so much of what we did to a three-ring circus.

*Flying Crane with Daisy Cutter Bomb, courtesy Wikipedia.org*

The company set up a perimeter around the mountaintop and everyone began digging in. I found a spot near the top where

I had quick and easy access to the new LZ. We were on hill 400 of Mutter's Ridge.

For the next several days, life for me on the hill was easy and routine. While three platoons of the company went on patrols around the hill looking for the enemy, I took it easy, brought in an occasional resupply helicopter, and just monitored the radio. I wrote letters home, spent hours talking with the artillery and mortar FO's, and ate. And of course, Terry and I spent countless hours talking about home, cars, girls, good food, and being back in the world. We had become good friends.

Bravo Company was then flown in to take control of the hill which would become battalion headquarters. Alpha Company pushed westward. Our objective was hill 484. We would first secure the hill; then engineers, who would travel with us, would blow the trees from the hill so that an LZ could be built. Once the LZ became accessible, the engineers would clear additional trees from the west side of the mountaintop and have a bulldozer brought in so that artillery gun pits could be built. Hill 484 would become a "Fire Support Base" (FSB) and would provide artillery support for the battalion both on this operation as well as on any future operations in the area.

As the company moved out, I took my position in the line with the rest of the company CP. Patrols had been sent out days earlier to scout the objective for possible enemy positions and to create a trail. Nothing was found that indicated the enemy had even been in this area. So this would be an easy hump if not for the heat. I was prepared to work any medivac choppers needed as I downed two salt tablets with another swig of hot water from my canteen.

The hike was only 1 kilometer, 1000 meters, and in normal terrain would have taken less than an hour. Due to the jungle and mountainous terrain, not to mention the intense heat, it took over four hours to move the company to the new hill. I had consumed half of my water, so a resupply chopper would be my first objective once the engineers had cleared the hill and created an LZ.

The engineers went right to work once the company secured the hill and formed a perimeter. They used C-4, a plastic explosive that was flexible like clay. They tied several sticks of the explosive around each tree, and ran a fuse from one stick to the next. When it was time to blow the explosives, we all had to move off the hill several hundred meters so that we would not be hit by any flying debris.

"Fire in the hole!" The familiar phrase went down the line alerting everyone to the impending detonation. Seconds later, an enormous explosion went off on the hilltop. Once it was over, we moved back up to the top of the hill. The hill was clear but not bare. The explosives had shattered each tree at ground level causing them to topple over, one by one. The stumps remained in the ground. Debris from the shattered trees made it difficult to move around. Now, the hill was covered with fallen trees that looked like a pile of pick-up sticks; but the jungle was open now, and the hill was accessible to a chopper.

It wasn't long before I received a call from a chopper alerting me that he was inbound with a bulldozer. The dozer was slung from a cable beneath the CH-46. It would be lowered onto the top of the hill where it would be used to push the debris and fallen trees off to the side. Then, they would start clearing the area where the gun pits would be dug.

The grunts dug in and set out listening posts and an ambush around the hill. Once I brought in the chopper, I followed the company CP to a location the CO had picked; and we all began digging our foxholes. In spite of the long exhausting day we had endured, everyone kept busy preparing their positions while the engineers went right to work building the new FSB.

By the end of the second day on Hill 484, the gun positions were ready. The hill had taken on a new look entirely. The gun pits were dug along the western ridgeline. All of the trees around the pits had been cleared so that the guns would have a clear field of fire for a full 360°. Now the attention turned to me since it was my task to bring in the choppers that were carrying the six 105 millimeter howitzers. Each gun was slung from a cable hanging from the bottom of the CH-46 chopper.

*Fire Support Base, Hill 484*

I had to direct each chopper with special arm movements to get the guns into position in the center of the pit where the cable would then be released. Once all of the guns had been dropped, additional choppers dropped slung nets with cases of ammunition into each gun pit. Finally, several CH-46's landed in the LZ, one at a time, carrying the gun crews for each gun. By day's end, the guns were firing their first mission, preparation for our movement to the next mountaintop, Hill 461, about one mile west of us. So far our trek along Mutter's Ridge had been an uneventful one – no sign of the enemy at all.

In the days to come, Alpha Company sent out patrols down the ridge that extended west towards Hill 461. On September 4th, a patrol found numerous pieces of NVA equipment and ammunition about 600 meters to the west of the FSB. Some unfinished bunkers were also found. The NVA were definitely in the area.

Then, on September 7th, an Alpha Company patrol made contact with two NVA soldiers as the patrol reached farther down the ridgeline towards Hill 461. The next day, the patrol moved down the ridgeline again and soon encountered a squad of NVA on the hilltop just east of Hill 461. More bunkers and equipment were found. It was becoming clear that we might soon be engaged in another major battle. All of the warning signs were there.

# CHAPTER

# *ELEVEN*

## BATTLE FOR HILL 461

D uring the first week in September, Alpha Company sent out daily patrols following the ridgeline westward towards what would be our next objective, Hill 461. I was never required to go on these platoon-size maneuvers. Instead, I stayed close to my radio and the company CP just in case air support was needed. I landed a few resupply helicopters each day but spent most of my time writing letters home, talking with my friends or catching some "Z's."

Again, Terry and I spent a lot of our free time talking about ourselves, what we did before Vietnam, and what we wanted to do when we got back to the world. We dreamed about new sporty cars like the Ford Mustang, Chevy Camaro, and Pontiac Firebird. We both wanted to get sporty car when we got home, and talking about it gave us a sort of incentive to get out of the Nam alive and safe.

Like all good things in Vietnam. Our short period of relaxation on Hill 484 came to an end. On September 7th, the company moved down the ridgeline which patrols had scouted out earlier. We were headed for the mountaintop that was Hill 461 where another LZ was to be built, LZ Sierra. We would follow the ridgeline westward so the hike wasn't expected to take long or to be very difficult. We would actually be walking downhill a good part of the way. Meanwhile, Bravo Company would take over our position and provide perimeter guard for the artillery battery.

As we moved out in single file, I radioed for an aerial observer to scout ahead of us for possible enemy positions. Patrols sent out days earlier had turned up bunkers, equipment, and small engagements. The point man moved slowly down a trail that had been created by these earlier patrols. Behind him, stretched 150 Marines in single file, keeping a spacing of about 10 meters between each other. Since our objective was about 2000 meters away, this meant that the point man would reach the objective while the last man had barely left our old position. Because of the terrain and dense jungle, it was the only way we could maneuver.

Progress was slow. The AO scouted ahead and to the north and south of us but saw nothing suspicious, partly because the jungle was so dense that it was nearly impossible to see the jungle floor. The AO soon departed, heading south to support another unit that had made enemy contact not far from the Rockpile.

By mid-afternoon we had reached the next hilltop, which lay less than 1000 meters from our objective. The ridgeline curved westward to north from this hill. The CO knew that sending the entire company forward was slowing our progress, so he decided to send one platoon ahead with hopes of securing Hill 461 before dusk. The remaining platoons and company CP would join the lead platoon the next day.

As the lead platoon continued to move westward, the rest of us dropped our gear and began to dig in for the night. The hill we were on had been bombed recently, probably in preparation for this operation. It wasn't bare; but many large trees were knocked down leaving tree trunks and debris scattered everywhere and making it difficult to move around and to dig in. I found a spot near the top of the hill and went to work digging my foxhole.

It wasn't long before shots rang out from the lead platoon. They had walked into an enemy ambush in the same vicinity where an earlier patrol had encountered two NVA soldiers. The fighting escalated quickly, and the company CP struggled to get dug in so that our 60 millimeter mortar crew could provide fire support for the engaged platoon. The CO didn't want to take any chances with just one platoon at point and the day coming to an end. He ordered the lead platoon to hold tight until he could confer with battalion headquarters.

I asked the CO if he wanted an aerial observer; but, given the denseness of the jungle and approaching darkness, he felt it would be a waste of resources. Soon, word came from battalion headquarters that we were to take up a defensive position for the night and continue operations in the morning. The lead platoon was ordered to return to the current company position. It was then that I learned that they had taken casualties, three killed and six wounded. But I had no LZ for landing a helicopter, and the wounded were not so serious that they needed to be medivaced immediately.

Terry and I decided to dig a hole together. Our position was just off a small trail we had created as the company moved into position on the hill. The platoons took up positions about 30 meters outward from this position forming a perimeter round the CP. The remainder of the day was calm as the lead platoon arrived back at our position and took up position on the west side, looking out at the ridgeline from which they had just come.

As night descended upon us, a listening post was put out about 100 meters down that ridgeline, since this was the most likely avenue for an enemy attack. I wasn't sure how well I would be able to sleep tonight knowing that we were now definitely in enemy territory. We had no idea of the strength of the enemy, whether it was just a few troops meant to harass us or a larger, more formidable force meant to attack and defeat us.

The CO put the platoons on 50% alert. That meant that at least one man in every two-man foxhole would be awake at all times. Men would take four hour shifts until dawn.

I had fallen sound asleep when, just before dawn, automatic weapons fire erupted on our western line. The shots came from the area from which we had expected an attack.

I dove into the foxhole, and Terry followed right behind me. The automatic weapons fire continued to come from our west. It was incoming fire, but it sounded like friendly fire and not the familiar AK-47 fire we had become accustomed to.

I quickly put on my flak jacket and helmet and tried to cock my 45 caliber pistol to chamber a round, but the gun jammed. I couldn't see in the darkness to fix it, so I pulled a hand grenade from my flak jacket. Terry still had an M-16, and he quickly chambered a round and clicked the safety off.

The automatic weapons fire continued to come from our west, and it was getting closer. Whoever it was behind that weapon, he was inside our perimeter and headed our way. I pulled the pin from my grenade and I held it tightly in my hand, keeping the spoon depressed, ready to throw. It was my only defense. If that man came down the trail by our foxhole, I was going to toss the grenade out at him.

This was the closest encounter I had had with the enemy, and I was scared to death. It was pitch dark, and I had no idea how many NVA were inside our perimeter. I couldn't distinguish an NVA soldier from one of our own in the darkness.

Muzzle flashes were still coming from the west and sporadic firing continued for several minutes, ours as well as the enemies. A few grenades went off. There was machine gun fire, and the situation was confusing in the noisy darkness.

Suddenly, we began taking incoming, 81 millimeter mortars. As I listened for the pop of the tubes, I realized that the pop was coming from the east. I could see flashes in the night sky from Hill 484. The incoming was our own. The mortar FO had called a fire mission onto our own position. I later learned that the CO ordered the mission. Since we were in our foxholes while the enemy wasn't, his thought was that the enemy was more likely to be hit by the mortars than our own men were.

The NVA soldier who had been spraying the area earlier with his automatic weapon had moved on. Evidently the CO's plan had worked; and as daybreak came, the NVA force had vanished back into the jungle.

I put the pin back into my grenade. The worst was over for now. As men began crawling out of their foxholes, information on what had happened quickly got back to those of us in the CP. One of the grunts manning an M-60 machine gun position had fallen asleep and the NVA over-ran his position capturing the machine gun and turning it on us. The sleeping Marine had been killed by his own weapon. Fortunately, in the darkness, no one else had been wounded or injured. I now had another routine medivac to get out, but there was no place to land a helicopter. He would have to wait.

Scuttlebutt travels fast, and the rumor was that there must be a tunnel complex nearby. That would explain how the NVA managed to slip past our listening post, attack us, and then disappear so easily. No enemy bodies or equipment were found. They were ghosts in the night.

The company remained on full alert for several hours before battalion headquarters gave the order to move out and take our final objective, Hill 461. Two platoons of grunts moved down the ridgeline they had traveled the day before. The sun was already making the day another hot one; the temperature quickly rose from a typical nighttime coolness of 90 degrees to over 100 degrees. I sensed it was going to be a busy day for air support, so I turned on my radio and called battalion to check communications.

"Candy Tuff one four, this is Alpha one four. Commo check, over."

"Ahh, roger, Alpha, five by, over."

"Roger that. I have you same, out."

Communications was good, and I guessed my radio battery would last another day. At least I hoped it would because I had no backup. Also, I wasn't sure when or where I might be able to land a resupply chopper. I had ordered two more batteries, but they hadn't been sent out yet.

Suddenly, Crack! Crack! Crack! Our two platoons had made enemy contact. They hadn't moved more than a hundred meters or so down the ridge when they came under fire. Word came down the line that there were wounded, so I grabbed my radio and weapon and went in search of the company commander, First Lieutenant Andrews, to see what I could do.

"We're going to need an LZ, Hunt. We've got a lot of wounded. See what you can do, find an LZ, and tell me what you need. We've got C-4 so we can blow trees if we have to, but we've got to be able to get birds in here."

"Roger that skipper. I'll get 'em in."

The hilltop was covered in debris from broken trees. The jungle was so dense that the bombs just knocked the trees over but did little to clear them from the hill. At the very top of the hill it was clearest. Although I knew there wasn't enough room to land a chopper, I felt that one could at least set its tail wheels down and lower its gate. The zone would have to be here; but the clearing was narrow, and I didn't think a chopper's rotors could clear the trees on each side. I also didn't like the fact that this hilltop was the most visible area around, making it a prime target for enemy fire.

As I looked around the perimeter of the hilltop, I could see Hill 461 directly across and to the west. It was only a thousand meters away, as the crow flies. If there were NVA on that mountaintop, which was likely, they could easily hit a helicopter trying to land on this hill, using mortars or other crew-served weapons such as recoilless guns or large machine guns. I didn't like it, but there was no other position close by that was even remotely large enough and clear enough to land a helicopter. Unless we had engineers brought in with equipment and lots of explosives, this was going to have to do. I just needed to have some of the outer trees blown down to be sure that a chopper's rotors would have ample clearance.

I reported back to the CO what I had decided, and he called one of his platoon leaders to have some men blow the trees. I pointed out which ones I wanted blown down. Meanwhile, the fighting had intensified. The two platoons left behind were now reduced to one as another platoon moved down the ridgeline to reinforce the engaged platoons. This was developing into another major battle. The wounded were mounting, and I knew that resupply and medivac choppers would need to land soon.

"Hunt, get an AO up here so I can get a better idea of what we're up against!"

"Roger skipper! Candy Tuff one four, this is Alpha one four. Request an AO, ASAP, over!"

"Roger, Alpha, out."

While I waited for the AO to arrive, I took up my position on top of the hill and began digging a foxhole right in the middle of the new LZ. A couple of the grunts who had been sent to blow the trees helped to remove the loose debris and tree limbs from the landing zone area. Soon I had the LZ up and ready to receive aircraft.

"Alpha one four, this is Bulldozer X-ray, over."

"Bulldozer X-ray, this is Alpha one four. We've got enemy contact at grid six two zero, niner five two, over."

"Roger, Alpha. I'll take a look."

An OV-10 Bronco approached overhead. This was a new aircraft which had just recently started operating in Vietnam in a reconnaissance role. The plane carried two pods of 60 millimeter rockets and six M-60 machine guns. The plane was reminiscent of the World War II aircraft P-38 with two tail booms jutting aft from the wing, one on each side. The OV-10 was much faster than the older O-1 Cessna, and it carried more fire power.

"One four man up!" the CO yelled out. I made my way down the backside of the LZ to see what he wanted.

"Hunt, I need that medivac chopper now. First platoon is sending back wounded. They need water and ammo as well. Get me a chopper NOW!"

"Yes sir!"

The CO turned to Terry who was his radio operator. "Terry, get the four on the line, tell him I need 5,000 rounds of ammo and a sling of water, ASAP."

"Roger that, skipper," Terry replied. As he radioed the battalion supply officer to request the needed supplies, I began walking back up the hill to the LZ and radioed battalion for a medivac chopper.

"Candy Tuff one four, this is Alpha one four, over."

"Alpha, this is Candy Tuff, over."

"Candy Tuff, request a routine medivac, over."

"Roger that, Alpha. Routine medivac, out."

"Alpha one four, this is Bulldozer X-ray, over."

"Go ahead, Bulldozer."

"Ah roger, Alpha. I've got what looks like a bunker complex on Hill 461. I buzzed the hill to take a closer look and took some small arms fire. I'm calling in an airstrike. What's the coordinates of your closest people, Alpha?"

"Wait one, let me check, Bulldozer." I stopped in my tracks and turned heading back down the hill to talk to the CO again.

"Skipper, the AO says he's got a bunker complex on Hill 461. Wants to call in an airstrike, but he needs to know where our people are."

"Tell him grid coordinates niner five two, six two one. Make sure he uses a run in heading of two one five, Hunt."

I took out my map to get a fix on those coordinates. It was just west of our position and about 500 meters from Hill 461. We could use 500 pound bombs and napalm on the hill, but the bursting radius would be close. Given the denseness of the jungle, I felt that this ordinance would still be safe for our troops.

"Bulldozer X-ray, Alpha one four. We've got friendlies at coordinates niner five two, six two one. Use a run in heading of two one five. Snake and nape but nothing larger, over."

"Ah roger, Alpha, understand. Snake and nape, run in two one five. I'll call it in."

I headed back up the hill to the LZ to finish my foxhole. By the time I had dug it about three feet deep, I got another call on the radio.

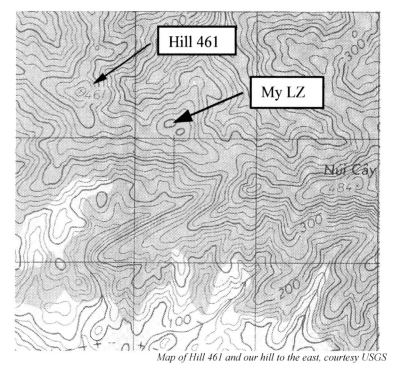

Hill 461

My LZ

*Map of Hill 461 and our hill to the east, courtesy USGS*

"Alpha one four, this is Badger Whiskey, over."

"Badger Whiskey, this is Alpha one four, over."

"One four, I'm inbound with crates of supplies and will pick up your wounded, what's your position, over."

"Badger Whiskey, I have you in sight, I'm at your two o'clock, flashing mirror, over."

"Ah roger, I have your mirror. What is your zone like, over?"

"Not good, Badger. It's a small zone, minimal clearance. I need you to fly north and east of my position, then come south down the valley, that is west of my position. You'll have to back into the zone and set your tail down. I'll guide you. We have friendlies to the southwest of this position. I have Bulldozer X-ray on station handling an airstrike on Hill 461, the next hill west of this position. His run in heading is two one five, over."

"Ah roger, Alpha, understand the LZ is hot, over?"

"Negative, LZ is not hot, but friendlies at coordinates niner five zero, six two one. Suspected bunker complex on Hill 461, over."

"Ah, roger."

The chopper could not fly directly into the zone from east to west because of large trees and debris on the east slope. The west slope was clear, and the wind direction was such that he could only come into the zone from the west.

As the chopper approached, I dropped my radio and began using arm signals to guide the pilot. His door gunner leaned out the door to see me. As I signaled move left or right or come straight back, the gunner in turn relayed the signals over the internal radio so the pilot could make corrections. The chopper was facing west but had to sit his tail wheels down on the LZ which was behind him. It was a tricky maneuver even in the best of conditions.

As the chopper eased backwards, I continued to check his rotor clearance on each side. His rotors had just a few feet of clearance. If I didn't guide him correctly and his rotors hit a tree, he would crash in the LZ. Then we'd never be able to get another chopper in.

Crack! Crack! Crack! Crack! Suddenly, I heard gunfire coming straight at us. It was a large gun, 50 caliber machine gun probably. The bullets whizzed past me. I jumped into my foxhole and grabbed the radio microphone keying it as I shouted above all the noise from the chopper.

"Get out of the zone! Get out of the zone! Get out of the zone!" I yelled. The pilot heard me and lifted rapidly straight up and to the north.

The gunfire had stopped as soon as the chopper left the LZ.

"Alpha one four, this is Badger, over."

"Badger this is Alpha, you were taking machine gun fire from Hill 461, over."

"Roger that, I could see the muzzle flashes."

"Badger, this is Bulldozer X-ray. I've got a flight of Phantoms on their way with snake and nape. Let me light up that hill, and then you can try it again, over."

"Roger Bulldozer, we'll hover to the southeast to stay out of your way."

"One four man up." The skipper was calling me again so I grabbed my radio and headed back down the hill to his position.

"Hunt, what's going on? Why didn't that chopper land? I've got wounded backed up, and I need to get them out of here. Was our ammo and water on that bird?"

"Skipper, there's a 50 cal machine gun on Hill 461. It opened fire the minute he tried to land. The AO's getting ready to run an airstrike of snake and nape to take it out. We'll try again as soon as the airstrike's over."

"Just do what you have to, but get that chopper in or some of these men are gonna die!"

I humped back up the hill just as two F-4 Phantoms streaked out of the sky and dropped a load of napalm and 500 pound snake eye bombs on Hill 461. That ought to take care of that machine gun.

"Alpha one four, this is Bulldozer X-ray, over."

"Bulldozer, this is Alpha, over."

"Let's try and get that chopper in again, over."

"Roger that, Badger Whiskey. This is Alpha one four, over."

"Go ahead, Alpha."

"Let's try it again Badger. Same deal as before, over."

"Roger, Badger is inbound."

The chopper swung north and east of my position. I prepared to signal him as I had done before, setting my radio down next to my foxhole and standing beside it. Bulldozer X-ray swooped down towards Hill 461 and released a volley of 60 millimeter rockets and M-60 machine gun fire. The chopper swung south now coming down the same valley. As it approached my LZ, it slowed to a hover and rotated its tail section around. The door gunner leaned out of the door watching for my hand signals.

I signaled to come straight back, holding both arms straight out in front of me, then bending them at the elbows and moving them back and forth.

The chopper slowly moved backwards, its wheels now about 20 feet from the hill and 6 feet off the ground. I stretched both arms straight out to my sides, then bent my right arm at the elbow and moved it back and forth touching my right shoulder. This signal meant that the pilot needed to move the chopper to my left.

Crack! Crack! Crack! Crack! I jumped back down into my foxhole grabbing the radio microphone, keying it and yelling "Get out of the zone! Get out of the zone! Get out of the zone!"

The noise was deafening from the chopper's engines and rotors, but I could still hear distinctly the crack of the 50 caliber machine gun on Hill 461 and the bullets zipping past my head. The air-strike didn't work. The machine gun was still there.

The chopper lifted up and quickly left the zone, heading north again to swing around and out of the area. I headed back down the hill to talk to the skipper and see what he wanted me to do next.

"Skipper, that gun is still there. I think we need more air support. What if I got some gunships and tried a coordinated attack with the gunships and an airstrike?"

"Hunt, I don't care what you've got to do; but get that damn chopper in this zone! We're out of ammo, we're out of water, we've got dozens of wounded and we're in danger of being overrun. I've called battalion for reinforcements and Bravo is on their way. Our platoons are pulling back to the perimeter. Where the hell is Terry?"

"Okay skipper, I'll get him in this time, and I'll find Terry."

I headed back up the hill to the LZ. The corpsman was heading down the hill.

"Hey doc, you seen Terry?"

"Yeah man, I just tagged him."

"What do ya' mean, you tagged him?"

"I tagged him damn it; he's dead. Took two 50 cals to the head."

I couldn't believe what I had just heard. Terry was dead. My best friend was dead. I had just seen him 15 minutes ago with the skipper, and now he was dead. When I got to the top of the hill, his body was covered with a poncho, just a few feet from where I had been standing as I guided the chopper. I had been so engrossed in trying to get that chopper into the LZ, I hadn't noticed that Terry had run up to help me by trying to spot the exact position of the machine gun on Hill 461. The thought that my best friend had just been killed trying to help me, trying to help all of us brought a lump to my throat. But I had to concentrate. I had to get that chopper into the LZ.

"Candy Tuff one four, this is Alpha one four, over."

"Alpha, Candy Tuff, over."

"Request immediate gunship support, over."

"Roger that, Alpha, out."

"Bulldozer X-ray, this is Alpha one four, over."

"Go ahead, Alpha."

"I've just asked for gunship support. Here's what I want to do. When the gunships arrive, I want to have them attack that hill on a heading of three six zero. I want you to have the Phantoms attack the hill with a run in of two one five. Badger will come up the middle and land just as he tried to before, over."

"Roger Alpha, but can you get another radio to talk to those gunships on a different frequency so we can keep the chatter on this frequency to a minimum? Things could get dicey real fast; and too much chatter will only confuse things more, over."

"Roger Bulldozer, good idea. Let me see what I can do, out."

I turned and hurried back down the hill to talk to the skipper, my radio on my back.

"Skipper, I need another radio to run this attack."

"Take mine. Doc just told me Terry was dead. Now I gotta find a new radio operator."

I grabbed Terry's radio, and slung it over my shoulder, and started back up the hill to the LZ.

"Alpha one four, this is Binder Delta, over."

"Binder Delta, this is Alpha, over."

"Ah, roger. Understand you need some gunship support. What do ya' have for us, over?"

"Ah roger, Binder, can we switch to a different frequency? Go to one niner, over?"

"Roger, Alpha, switching to one niner, out."

I changed the frequency on Terry's radio to 19, so I could talk to the gunships separately from the AO and the medivac chopper.

"Binder Delta, how do you read, over?"

"Roger, Alpha. Five by, over."

"Okay Binder, I've got a 50 cal machine gun on Hill 461. I've got a 46 (CH-46 chopper) with supplies and ready to take out wounded hovering to my south. I'm at your three o'clock flashing mirror. Bulldozer X-ray is on station controlling airstrikes on the hill. I need you to lay down suppressing rockets and machine guns at the same time Bulldozer runs the airstrike. Your run in is three six zero. Wait till I give the command before you attack. I've got another radio to talk to Bulldozer and the 46. Any questions, over?"

*M2 Machine gun, 50 caliber, courtesy Wikipedia.org*

"Roger, Alpha, understand. Target is Hill 461, run in is three six zero. Wait for your command."

I called the AO and chopper to set up the attack and landing.

"Bulldozer X-ray, this is Alpha one four, over."

"Go ahead, Alpha."

"Roger, I've got Binder Delta hovering to the south, ready to run their attack. Badger Whiskey, this is Alpha one four, over."

"Roger, Alpha, I monitored. I'm moving into position."

The Huey gunships flew in a tight circle a hundred meters or so above the treetops, just to my southeast. The CH-46 swung northward, still to the east of my position. The OV-10 Bronco swooped down from the northeast heading straight for Hill 461. As he approached the hill, he fired a Willie Pete rocket which exploded with a bright flash from the burning phosphorous; and a white cloud of smoke rose up from the mountaintop. Overhead I could hear the F-4 Phantoms circling, preparing to make a bomb run on the target that was just marked by the Bronco.

I keyed the microphone of the radio on my back. "Bulldozer X-ray, you're a go. Badger Whiskey, you're a go." Then I keyed the microphone of the other radio. "Binder Delta, you're a go."

Like an orchestra rising to a crescendo to the swing of a conductor's arm, the aircraft descended upon their target. The first Huey unleashed a wave of 20 millimeter rockets from each of his two rocket pods, while his six M-60 machine guns fired in rapid succession. When he reached a distance of about 500 meters from the target, he dropped and peeled off to the south so the second Huey could repeat this performance.

Two F-4 Phantom jets streaked down from the northeast heading diagonally towards the target. Just before reaching the hill, the first jet released four 500 pound canisters of napalm, which tumbled gently towards the ground before erupting in four enormous but distinct balls of fire. The second jet wasn't far behind, diving at the fireballs and releasing four 500 pound snake eye bombs. As the bombs descended towards the mountaintop, the CH-46 came down the valley flying low, just above the treetops. He timed his arrival perfectly, arriving at a position between my LZ and Hill 461 just after the bombs had impacted and thrown their shrapnel out and around the point of impact.

The jets ascended back up into the sky as the chopper slowed and then hovered, rising to a point that was level with the

LZ. The Hueys circled around and made a second pass at Hill 461 unleashing another volley of rockets and machine gun fire.

I dropped my radio and stood at the center of the hill, my arms outstretched as I began to guide the chopper backwards. Again, the noise from the rotors made it difficult to hear; and dust and debris kicked up and pelted me in the face.

Six feet, five feet, four feet...the chopper's tail wheels touched the hill for a brief moment, then rose again. For an instant I feared he was going to lift up into the air and leave, but he was only making some corrections before setting his tail wheels on the ground. The tailgate lowered, and several grunts who waited with wounded ran aboard to help unload the crates of supplies, ammunition and water.

Except for the noise from the chopper, it was calm and quiet. There was no enemy fire. The combined airstrikes had worked. Not only had the 50 caliber machine gun been knocked out, but the hill was becoming more and more barren from the repeated assaults.

Our platoons had made it back to our hill, and the chopper was loaded with wounded soldiers. After lifting off and returning to Dong Ha to drop off the wounded, the chopper pilot made several more trips back to the hill to take out more wounded. Each time he returned, I had to hand guide him onto the hill.

It was September 8th. The wounded were evacuated first. When the chopper returned to take out the dead, the reality of Terry's death began to hit me. His body lay on the ground with a poncho covering it. When the chopper approached this time, prop wash from his rotors blew the poncho off. The sight was sickening. Half of Terry's head was blown away from the two 50 caliber bullets that had struck him down. At least he didn't suffer; death came instantly.

Bulldozer X-ray continued to run airstrikes on Hill 461 and the surrounding area. The Hueys returned to Quang Tri, reloaded, and came back to strafe the ridgeline some more under the control of Bulldozer X-ray. I spent the remainder of the day getting the wounded and dead Marines out to safety and treatment.

As darkness approached, what was left of Alpha Company remained alert, anticipating another ground attack. Bravo Company arrived shortly after dark and dug in with us to reinforce our perimeter. That night the Bravo one four man ran a Spooky Gunship mission. The large, slow flying aircraft lit up the sky over Hill 461 as its 20 millimeter cannons tore up the ground all around the hill and the ridgeline that led to it from our position.

The next day, what was left of Alpha Company marched back to the FSB where we were lifted off the hill and returned to the Rockpile. Bravo Company moved down the ridgeline where we had been attacked. By the end of the day, I was at the Rockpile eating hot chow when I got the word that Bravo had reached Hill 461 after an intense battle on the hill. What NVA were left had faded back into the jungle.

In that one day of combat, Alpha Company had sustained so many casualties that we had to be pulled out of the battle. Alpha would have to wait for replacements before it would be combat ready again. We also got a new company commander, Captain Shaw.

The loss of Terry was devastating. I never learned his real name, but that was the Nam, and that was the Corps. It wasn't unusual to know someone by a nickname or their last name only. Terry was the first good friend I had made since my arrival in Vietnam. His death seemed unreal to me, and I would mourn the loss for the remainder of my tour and remember our brief friendship for the rest of my life.

# CHAPTER
# *TWELVE*
## INTO THE DMZ

In October, 1968, we received new orders for an operation called Lancaster II. We were going into the DMZ. We would spend most of the month moving from mountaintop to mountaintop right up to the Ben Hai River. I had been transferred back to H & S Company, Battalion Headquarters. I felt relieved. Being in the Battalion CP meant that I would not have to deal with the day-to-day activities of an infantry line company. Simply put, being a one four man in the battalion headquarters would be much easier.

The entire battalion entered the DMZ on October 8th. Each company was assigned an area to search out. The most important part of this mission was to destroy a 6,000 meter road that extended from the Ben Hai River, southward through the DMZ. The road had been used by the NVA to move artillery and personnel into the area so that they could be used to attack U.S. bases such as the Rock Pile and Camp Carroll, as well as to threaten larger bases at Dong Ha and Quang Tri. This was a major operation for the battalion, and we were expected to encounter a lot of enemy contact.

Where the road crossed the Ben Hai River, a stone bridge had been built just beneath the surface of the river. Delta Company would occupy Hill 200 which overlooked the river and the bridge. H & S Company would also occupy this hill, putting the battalion headquarters about as close to North Vietnam as you could get without actually entering it (about 1000 meters).

We occupied this hill from October 8$^{th}$ to October 22$^{nd}$. The other three companies occupied other hills close by, and patrols were sent out daily from all of the companies. The amount of supplies, ammunition, weapons, and bunkers found was staggering – weapons magazines, mortar rounds, helmets, ponchos, entrenching tools, grenades, RPG's, belts, underwear, gas masks, mortar fuses, TNT, picks, shovels, axes, batteries, crossbows, clothing, and even several enemy trucks. Our companies unearthed dozens of tunnel complexes, bunkers, artillery gun pits, anti-aircraft weapons pits, and connecting roads to these positions. The infiltration of the NVA was simply enormous.

The road that the NVA had built was hidden beneath the triple canopy of the jungle. Our mission was to destroy the road, destroy the tunnel and bunker complexes, and destroy the stone bridge. All captured equipment and supplies were sent to the rear; and we used the ammunition, especially artillery and mortar rounds, to blow up the road and open the jungle canopy, so any future attempt to repair the road could be observed by air support.

The road was 10 to 12 feet wide. Evidence showed that this road had been built entirely by hand. Tree roots along banks had been cut cleanly. If built by machinery such as a bulldozer, these roots would have been torn out. Gun pits had clean cut rectangular walls which could only have been cut by hand with shovels and picks. There was even a truck park near one enemy artillery position and three branch roads that led out to the different gun pits. These would have been used to move the artillery pieces into their positions.

The gun pits were 20 feet wide by 20 feet long. They had ramps leading down into them so that the guns could be easily brought in. They were well-camouflaged, using vines as the framework and tree saplings to provide cover. There were also ammo bunkers adjacent to the gun pits full of 152 millimeter and 107 millimeter shells.

Two destroyed Soviet artillery tractors had also been found. Both had 12-cylinder engines and special hitches that could be used to tow the artillery weapons. They had power winches as well and a towing capacity of 14 tons.

One company even found a small village of hooches, living quarters for approximately 200 NVA construction workers. There was another set of A-frame bunkers in the village which would have housed another 200 NVA soldiers. Also, seventeen graves were found.

The one thing the companies did not find was the enemy himself. There were some brief encounters with small elements of NVA but no major battles. However, all companies, including battalion headquarters, took incoming nearly every single day, many times from deep inside North Vietnam. Incoming ranged from very large artillery rounds such as 130 millimeter, to small mortars, such as 61 millimeter. The incoming made each day seem like an eternity because you knew it was coming, but you never knew when. No matter what I was doing, inside I was constantly aware of the possibility of taking incoming, and therefore spent all day waiting for it to happen. I made sure that, wherever I was, there was a foxhole nearby for me to jump into.

As the battalion one four man, I wasn't required to bring in any helicopters. My primary duties were to help the company one four men whenever they needed air support. I would relay their calls to regimental headquarters and help to coordinate the arrival and departure of aircraft that flew support for us. Often when we took incoming, I would call for an aerial observer; and I would work closely with the battalion FO to find out what the azimuth was to the gun that was firing on us. All too often the gun was deep inside North Vietnam, and the slow flying OV-10 Bronco pilots didn't want to venture too far north for fear that they might get shot down.

It was during these weeks on hill 200 that I met two Marines I will never forget. First, there was Corporal Colin Bach. Bach was a radio operator who worked in the battalion commo section. He had been through radio school in San Diego also, so we had that in common and often talked about our experiences there.

Being in battalion also meant being close to the air liaison officer, Lieutenant Wiley. Lieutenant Wiley was a helicopter pilot. He was to spend three months with the battalion before returning to his unit and flying choppers. He had been with us for two months when I met him, and he often talked about a job he had lined up to fly commercial airplanes once he returned from Vietnam. Although he was an officer, I got to know him during the many hours spent working with him.

It was during these weeks that I had entered my sixth month in Vietnam. Now, I was considered one of the seasoned veterans. I had experienced combat numerous times; and men like Bach, who was newer to the battalion, wanted to draw on my experience. Since Lieutenant Wiley was a chopper pilot, being in the field was a completely new experience for him. I worked with him several times when an aerial observer was on station searching surrounding areas. I would explain some of the radio transmissions to the

Lieutenant. Although he was a chopper pilot, he had little knowledge about how we used tactical air support when a combat situation arose. He was more accustomed to flying supplies out to a unit than engaging in offensive combat.

For the most part, our stay in the DMZ was not very eventful for me. Because I was assigned to the CP I did not have to go on patrols or get involved in the day-to-day search and destroy activities of the line companies. The CP did not change positions the way a company might, moving from one hill to another to broaden their search area. Since Delta Company was providing perimeter guard for the battalion CP, their one four man handled day-to-day air control such as choppers bringing in resupplies or taking out wounded. All of these things made my job rather routine, almost boring.

However, events of October 22, 1968, the day we were being lifted out of the DMZ and carried back to the Rockpile, became permanently etched in my mind and contributed extensively to the post traumatic stress I endured after I returned to the world. The helo lift began at approximately 11:30 a.m. The Delta one four man was coordinating the lift as I remained in the battalion CP monitoring the radio. I had a second radio by my side to talk to regimental command when necessary. Lieutenant Wiley, Major Reynolds (the operations officer), and an artillery FO, whose name I can't remember, were the officers who remained in the battalion CP during the lift. Bach and a few other enlisted men also remained in the CP. The CP was located about 100 meters down the hill on the south side and 100 meters up from the LZ.

About 30 minutes into the lift, we began taking incoming, 130 millimeter artillery from deep inside North Vietnam. The rounds were impacting below the battalion CP near the LZ where the choppers were landing. It appeared that the LZ was the intended target.

"Candy Tuff one four, this is Delta one four. Request immediate aerial observer, over."

"Roger, Delta, out. Fire Raider one four, this is Candy Tuff one four, over."

"Go ahead, Candy Tuff, over."

"Roger, Fire Raider. Request immediate aerial observer, over."

"Roger, Candy Tuff. We'll get right on it, out."

By the time the AO had arrived on station, we had taken six rounds of incoming. The rounds came one at a time in intervals of about five minutes. It seemed that every time the chopper would try to land, a round would be fired.

"Candy Tuff one four, this is Ram Rod Zulu, over."

"Roger, Ram Rod, this is Candy Tuff one four. We are taking incoming from azimuth zero three two, over."

"Roger, Candy Tuff, how big is it, over?"

"Big, Ram Rod. Probably 130's, over."

"What's your position, Candy Tuff?"

"Niner niner five, six niner five, over."

Knowing the size of the incoming and the azimuth would help the AO locate the gun that was firing on us. A 130 millimeter gun could shoot as far as 26 miles, which would put the gun deep inside North Vietnam. The azimuth I gave the AO was the direction from my position from which the shelling was coming. By knowing this information, the AO could get on a flight path that flew over our position and straight at the gun that was firing at us. If the azimuth was correct, he should be able to locate the gun and direct counterfire onto it.

Whomp! The deep, hollow sound of the gun came again, and round 7 was on its way. I had learned to recognize that sound many months ago, and my ears had become acutely trained to listen for it at all times. Because the artillery round traveled faster than the sound itself, you only had approximately 15 seconds from the time you heard the gun pop until the moment the round would impact. Those 15 seconds could mean the difference between living and dying. If you heard the tube pop, you might have time to reach cover such as a foxhole.

I had grabbed my two radios earlier when the first round was fired, and I took cover in a trench not far from my own foxhole. The trench was about six feet long, two feet wide, and four feet deep. When I jumped into the hole, Lieutenant Wiley, the artillery FO, and Major Reynolds jumped in with me. I was on the far right-hand side of the hole (facing south). Lieutenant Wiley was to my left. The artillery FO was next to Lieutenant Wiley, and Major Reynolds was on the far left hand side of the trench.

Another two-man foxhole was directly below our trench about 6 meters away. The only other foxhole nearby was my own which lay about 20 meters above and to the right of the trench.

This time the round impacted much closer to the battalion CP. It appeared that the enemy was beginning to walk the rounds up the hill. This was a standard procedure they often followed by slightly reducing the range of the gun each time so the impacts peppered the area.

"Ram Rod, this is Candy Tuff. We just took another round, same azimuth, over."

"Roger, Candy Tuff. I don't see anything yet; hang in there, Candy Tuff."

The AO was over the Ben Hai River heading north. The helicopter that was trying to land to take another load of men out made his approach again.

Whomp! Another round was fired and, again, impacted a little closer to our position. The fear of such large artillery was heart wrenching. Each round that was fired would sound like a speeding freight train as it roared over our heads and impacted down the slope of Hill 200.

Delta one four was on the other radio talking with the helicopter pilot and guiding him into the LZ. Because of the steepness of the hill, the pilot had to back into the LZ in the same manner as the choppers I had directed when we were fighting for Hill 461 a month earlier. That meant that Delta one four had to hand guide the chopper in until it could set its tail wheels onto the ground and lower its tailgate.

Whomp! Round 9 was on its way. This round came closer than any I had ever encountered, flying directly over the trench we were in. The sound was almost deafening as it screamed just above our heads impacting about 50 meters away. The sound of shrapnel pierced the air upon impact, and this scared the hell out of me. We were now in direct line of the gun. I knew this was not a good thing. I had to get out of this foxhole.

I stood up and looked around to see what other foxholes might be close by. The closest hole was just down from ours, but it was on the same trajectory of the gun, and two men already occupied that hole. I turned around facing north and saw my own foxhole 20 meters away. I started to climb out of the trench when I heard the gun pop again. Whomp!

I ducked back down into the hole and curled up into a tight fetal position. "Oh God, please don't let me get hit! Please God, please don't let me get hit!" I prayed. I'm not a religious person but there I was proving the old saying that "there are no atheists in foxholes." At that moment, I feared dying more than I had ever feared anything before. I knew that we were in the direct path of this gun and that the last round impacted just 50 or so meters away. If the enemy continued to walk the rounds up the hill, the next round would impact even closer.

I listened intently for the incoming round – that familiar freight train sound that you hear just before impact. But it was silent. For a moment I thought perhaps the "whomp" I heard wasn't the gun firing at us, but instead was counterfire from one of our own artillery batteries. As soon as that thought entered my mind, there was a loud ringing in my ears as dirt came pouring down on me.

"Oh God! Oh Jesus! Oh God, someone help me! Oh Jesus!"

Someone was screaming for help. Was I hit? What happened? I was stunned for a few seconds unaware that the incoming round had impacted on the lip of our foxhole. That explains why it was deathly silent just prior to the impact – you never hear the round that gets you because it is heading straight at you.

"Jesus! Someone help me! Oh God, it hurts, help me!"

It was Lieutenant Wiley; he was wounded. I was afraid to move, afraid that they would fire another round.

"Please, someone help me! Oh Jesus!"

I jolted to my senses and stood up to see what was wrong. Lieutenant Wiley's left arm was gone, torn off just above the elbow. His upper arm was swollen to twice its size. Fragments of bone were protruding from the torn flesh, and his blood spurted rhythmically to the beat of his heart.

"Do something, Hunt. I'm going to bleed to death! Oh God, it hurts so bad!"

Jolted into action by his words, I remembered what I had learned as a Boy Scout about using a tourniquet to stop severe bleeding. I took off my belt and wrapped it around his upper arm pulling it as tight as I could.

"Corpsman up! Corpsman up!" I yelled.

While all of this was happening, I had completely forgotten about my radios and the aerial observer.

"Candy Tuff one four, this is Ram Rod Zulu. Did you just take another round, over?"

I heard the AO calling me. I turned and looked for my radios. One of them had taken shrapnel in the side, but the one that the AO was calling me on was okay.

"Roger, Ram Rod. We did, over."

"Roger that. I've got the gun in sight. I'm about 20 miles inside North Vietnam. I have fixed-wing on station, and I'm calling in an airstrike."

I felt relieved. The aerial observer had taken a terrible chance flying that deep into North Vietnam, but he had found the gun. That meant we would probably not take any more incoming, at least not from that gun.

The corpsman arrived and went to work immediately on Lieutenant Wiley. Several other men arrived and began to help the major and the other lieutenant out of the foxhole. The artillery FO managed to climb out of the hole on his own, but then fell face first onto the ground. Shrapnel had pierced his helmet and was lodged in the back of his head.

The major had taken shrapnel in the back, and I later learned that he lost a kidney. Nearby was another casualty, my new friend Colin Bach. I saw him lying up against a tree about ten meters up the hill and to the left. I went over to help him. At the same time one of the corpsmen arrived with me.

"Let's take off his flak jacket, I think he's been hit in the chest," the corpsman said to me.

As I tried to unsnap the flak jacket, Bach's head rolled backward; and his helmet fell off revealing a large, gaping wound to his head. I was holding him in my arms when seconds later, the corpsman pronounced him dead. I had just lost another friend.

I was angry. I was sad. I felt sick to my stomach. In just a few short months I had made two good friends, and both were dead now. Both had been killed violently just yards from where I was. Both had been killed by severe head wounds, a world away from their homes and their families. I felt helpless and ashamed that I had survived. The emotional pain swelled up inside me, and the memories of these losses would remain with me for the rest of my life. I felt that I would never see my own family or home again. It was just a matter of time before I would be dead also.

I walked back down to the trench I had been in when the round impacted. They were loading Lieutenant Wiley onto a stretcher and were getting ready to carry him down to the LZ to be medivaced. His pain had subsided after the corpsman had administered morphine. An intravenous bottle of liquid was being held by another man, while two Marines carried the stretcher.

"Wait, I want my arm!" he cried ou.

There in the bottom of the hole lay his arm. A large Seiko watch was still strapped around the wrist. I jumped into the hole, retrieved the arm, and set it on his lap.

"Semper Fi, sir!"

"Semper Fi, Hunt, and thanks." he murmured.

That was the last time I would see Lieutenant Wiley, another friend I had made recently. That was the last round of incoming we took that day. The AO directed an airstrike on the gun and took it out. The remainder of the battalion was lifted off the hill and returned to the Rockpile. As my chopper landed there, we began taking incoming mortars. Wondering if this would ever end, I ran off the chopper and dashed for a bunker 20 or 30 meters away. However, the mortars turned out to be just a few rounds of harassing fire.

That evening, I was walking down to the shower point to wash the blood and dirt off of me. I had been in the DMZ for over 30 days, and I looked forward to being able to take a shower which did not happen very often. As I approached the shower stall, the battalion commander, Colonel Twohey, came out.

"Damn Hunt, did you get hit?" he asked, seeing the blood all over my jungle fatigues.

"No, sir, it's Lieutenant Wiley's blood. I was in the foxhole with him when he got hit. Sir, I've been here six months now, I need an R & R, sir." (R & R is rest and relaxation)

"There's a plane leaving for Tai Pei, Taiwan in a few days. Be on it, Hunt. You've earned it."

A couple of days later, I caught a resupply chopper back to Quang Tri. From there I hitch-hiked northward to the Dong Ha airfield where I caught a C-130 to Da Nang. There I spent a night waiting for a commercial airliner to take a group of us to Tai Pei. Men from all branches of the military on that plane, and the chatter about combat experiences echoed from one end to the other.

Tai Pei was an experience I'll always remember. My three days there fell right at the time of the presidential election back in the U.S. I met with a few men in the Army, and we quickly became friends. We used every hour of the day to do everything we could that would put the war out of our thoughts. We went to a movie dubbed in English. We ate at numerous restaurants, shopped in quaint stores which sold everything from knickknacks to expensive cameras and stereo equipment. One day we took a bus to tour a large dam.

Of course, most of us enjoyed the company of a young woman, even though we had to pay the equivalent of $75.00 to a "papasan" for her services.

It seems strange now looking back. The second night there, my girl rented a tuxedo for me and took me to a fancy restaurant, where I had the pleasure of meeting *her parents*. It was her 21$^{st}$ birthday, and they were throwing her a big party. In China, a person celebrates their birthday on the day that they were conceived. I was going to be 21 in January, so I was actually a little older than the girl. It was a great feeling to be at such a party, able to put the war so far behind me. She asked me what I wanted to eat for dinner. To my surprise, I asked for and received a big plate of spaghetti with meatballs. There was an orchestra, and we danced and had a great time. She was a sweet girl though, and all the while I couldn't help wondering if her parents knew what she did for a living.

On our last night there, we sat in one of our hotel rooms and listened to the Armed Forces Radio Network on the radio. It was election night. I was never one to take an interest in politics and didn't know the difference between a Democrat and a Republican at the time. It wasn't until that night that I learned that the Republican candidate, Richard Nixon based his campaign in part on the promise to end the war in Vietnam. So I was really excited to hear that he had won the election and would be our next President. I wanted to see this war end as quickly as possible, so no more young men would have to experience what I had experienced in just six short months.

The next day, a number of us met up at the U.S.O. club just hours before we had to go to the airport to catch a plane back to Vietnam. I was sitting at the bar drinking a Vodka Collins and talking with another soldier when he told me a bizarre story. He had a very large carving of a human hand giving the traditional symbol for "up yours" – the finger. He was half drunk and kept telling me how he and another fellow pulled off the "heist of the century." His friend had distracted a shop owner, while he tucked the carved hand under his shirt and slipped out of the store.

"Hey, there's my buddy now," he said. I turned and looked towards the door where an Army Chaplin was standing. I almost choked on my drink! Like I said, I'm not a religious person, but I definitely remember something about "Thou shall not steal" being in the bible – one of those 10 commandments I believe!

The next day I was on another C-130 headed back to Dong Ha. From there I hitchhiked to our rear at Quang Tri where I spent another night before catching a chopper back out to the Mutter's Ridge. As crazy as my R & R had been, it was depressing to return to the war zone after spending a few peaceful days back in "civilization."

CHAPTER

# *THIRTEEN*

## RETURN TO HILL 461

A fter my return from R & R, I was sent back to Alpha
Company. The battalion was once again assigned to
operations along Mutter's Ridge, but Alpha was
lifted back to Camp Carroll to provide perimeter guard for
the base. It was November, and the days were beginning to
get shorter. The 100 plus temperatures had receded to a
more comfortable and milder 90 degrees average.

It was nice to be in what was considered a "stand down"
situation. Camp Carroll was much better than being on
Mutter's Ridge. We had large tents to sleep in and real cots,
not the hard ground. Sandbagged bunkers were just outside
the tents, because the base made a good target for incoming
artillery and mortars. The best part about being at Camp
Carroll was the food – hot chow on a real plate and cold
milk. I had come to love the cold milk they served in the

messhall and would drink glasses and glasses of it every chance I got.

On November 13th, I was laying on my cot just taking it easy and enjoying the calmness of the day. I had just come back from the mess hall and some of the men in the tent were passing around cake to celebrate the birthday of the Marine Corps, November 10th. We were laughing and enjoying ourselves. Being at Camp Carroll for a few weeks was almost like being back in the world. It was relaxing, it was easy duty; and, after all that we had been through in the past 6 months, it was a relief.

The sounds of laughter were suddenly silenced by an explosion from the tent next to ours. Instinctively we all dashed out of our tent and jumped into the bunker outside. Anxiously we waited for more explosions because we all thought it was an artillery or mortar barrage. No explosions came, but moments later I heard another familiar sound.

"One four man up! One four man up!"

Someone had been wounded. Cautiously I left the bunker, then increased my pace running first back into my tent to retrieve my radio and then back out towards the tent next to ours.

"One four man up!" someone yelled from inside the other tent. I ran inside to find several men wounded from the explosion. I couldn't believe what I was seeing. The worst of the wounds was a man the corpsman was trying to treat. It appeared as though his entire backside, from the waist downwards was nothing but shredded meat.

"You the one four man?"

"Yes."

"I need an emergency medivac with AMA, ASAP!"

"What happened?" I asked.

"He sat on a grenade man, get me that medivac!"

"Candy Tuft one four, this is Alpha one four. Request emergency medivac with AMA ASAP! Over!"

An emergency medivac meant that the man could die any minute. "AMA" meant airborne medical assistance. The corpsman wanted a doctor onboard the medivac chopper to administer treatment to the wounded man while he was being taken to a hospital operating room.

Within minutes, a chopper was enroute to Camp Carroll from Quang Tri; but before he arrived the man died. As the story of what happened got out, it was difficult to believe. Four men were sitting around a cot in the tent next to mine, playing cards. One of them asked another Marine to toss him his flak jacket because he wanted to get a pack of cigarettes out of the pocket. When the other Marine picked up the flak jacket and tossed it, a grenade that was strapped to the jacket by the safety pin, fell off and rolled right to the area of the four men playing cards. The grenade was armed.

In an instant, one of the men grabbed his helmet, put it over the grenade, and sat on it to protect the other men. The grenade exploded literally blowing his ass away, turning him to hamburger from the waist down. Three other men were wounded, but none seriously.

This event shook me. Even when you think you're safe, you're not. I thought that being in a fortified position such as Camp Carroll made it safe. This incident just proved that you could not let your guard down even for a moment.

Weeks earlier, I had come as close to death as one could come when the artillery round impacted on the lip of the foxhole I was in. Up until that moment, I had become confident that if I heard the pop of an enemy gun, I would be safe if I made it to a foxhole. I structured my day-to-day life by being constantly on the alert to listen for that familiar pop and to know where the closest foxhole was.

It now appeared that my chances of surviving Vietnam were no better that day than they were the day I landed in country.

Even after six months of experience and combat, with all that I had learned about survival, there were still things beyond my imagination and beyond my control that could kill me.

Ironically enough, Alpha Company was air lifted by chopper to the FSB on Hill 484 the very next day, November 14th. We were going back to Hill 461, now called LZ Sierra. Since it had been given the status of a landing zone, I couldn't understand why we had to hump thousands of meters to get to it instead of just heloing to it.

The CO requested a recon of Hill 461 before the company was lifted to the FSB. The recon party consisted of the CO, his new radio operator, the artillery FO, the mortar FO, and me. We were picked up at Camp Carroll by a Huey Gunship. Moments later, we approached the ridgeline.

The chopper circled Hill 461 and the ridgeline that connected it to our previous position to the east. As the chopper banked to the right, I peered out of the open door and studied the terrain below. Although it had been over a month since friendly troops had been on the hill, I could see fresh trails weaving through the rubble of bombed out jungle. The remains of open NVA bunkers and foxholes could also be seen scattered around the top of Hill 461.

As we continued to circle the hill, I suddenly caught movement out of the corner of my eye. Swiftly turning my head to look closer, I could have sworn I saw a man jump into a foxhole as we passed overhead.

"Skipper! There's someone down there!" I yelled.

"Bullshit! There hasn't been anyone on this hill in a month, Hunt."

Since he was a Captain and I was only a Lance Corporal, I couldn't argue the point with him. I turned and looked at the other enlisted men to see what their reaction was and to see if anyone else saw this suspected enemy soldier. The mortar FO simply shrugged his shoulders as if to say, "Forget it man, what are you gonna do?"

The chopper headed east now. Minutes later we touched down on the FSB, Hill 484. The CO had his radio operator call battalion and request that the airlift begin. I took up a position on the LZ to coordinate the lift.

Once the entire company had arrived on Hill 484, we formed a single file down the western slope and prepared to move out. At least, the hump would be somewhat easier since there was now a pretty good trail between Hill 484 and our objective, Hill 461.

By late afternoon, we had reached the hill that Terry had given his life on. Hill 461 was still an hour's walk from here. Because the day was coming to an end, the CO decided to send just one platoon ahead with the intent of sending the remainder of the company the next morning.

As the sun sank lower and lower casting deep shadows across the terrain, we all began clearing out old foxholes and setting up our defensive position for the night. It wasn't long before shots rang out from Hill 461.

Instinctively, I grabbed my radio, called for an aerial observer, and moved to a position behind a tree stump where I could get a better view of the mountaintop. I could hear explosions on Hill 461, and I could see black smoke rising from them.

The CO joined me by the tree stump and briefed me on the situation that was rapidly developing. The advance platoon had reached the objective. Not seeing any sign of the enemy, they had dropped their gear. They were taking a few minutes to rest before setting up their defensive position for the night, when they were ambushed by NVA soldiers occupying the same position.

The soldier I had seen earlier was an NVA. The NVA were using the foxholes and bunkers we had seen as we circled the hill just hours before during our reconnaissance mission. The NVA often used a trick to give the appearance that the foxholes were empty. They tied woven bamboo mats to their backs. The mats were caked with mud and dirt and made it appear that the hole was empty when they crouched down in the hole creating a false bottom.

*Hill 461*

As soon as our platoon had let down their guard and dropped their gear, the NVA sprang their attack, popping up from the holes and unleashing a barrage of AK-47 fire while setting off claymore mines (our own captured mines) that were tied in broken tree trunks. NVA snipers were in trees surrounding the hill. The attack came swiftly and with deadly fire. The platoon made a rapid retreat back down the ridgeline which connected to our hill, dragging their dead and wounded with them.

The skipper had been talking to the platoon leader, a young lieutenant to get more details about what had just happened. The situation rapidly became confusing, and it was questionable whether all of our men got off the hill.

"Hunt, get me an airstrike of snake and nape on that hill, now!"

"Yes sir!"

"Alpha one four, this is Bulldozer X-ray, over."

The same AO I had used before when we were in this area was now on station. That was a good thing, I thought, because he would already be familiar with the terrain.

"Go ahead Bulldozer, over."

"What have you got Alpha?"

"Ambush on Hill 461. I need a strike of snake and nape. Use a run in of two one five. Closest friendlies are six two one, niner five two, over."

"Roger, Alpha. I copy run in two one five."

The shooting had stopped on Hill 461. The CO sent another platoon out a hundred meters or so to set up our own ambush, in case the NVA tried to pursue the fleeing platoon. The remainder of the company formed a perimeter around our hill. I stuck close to the CO to see what other kind of air support he might want.

Soon, a flight of Phantoms was circling overhead. The AO set himself in a position that would allow him to mark the target with a Willie Pete rocket. For a brief moment, I had lost track of the AO, where he was, and what he was doing. Suddenly, I heard one of his rocket pods fire and heard the rocket streaking straight for our position. Instinctively, I ducked. In an instant the rocket impacted about 50 meters east of me.

"Abort! Abort! Abort!" I screamed into the microphone. I knew that this rocket was meant to mark the target and that within seconds two F-4 Phantom jets would be streaking down from the sky and unleashing napalm and 500 pound bombs, on us!

"Sorry, Alpha, I had a hot pod, didn't mean to mark that position."

A hot pod meant that the rocket had fired prematurely. Realizing that he had just marked our position for the jets, the AO reacted instinctively and radioed the jets to disregard the marking rocket.

"Bulldozer, could you change your run in for target marking to two one five, over?" I requested.

"Roger that, Alpha. Sorry 'bout that."

The OV-10 circled the area and came back around to the northeast so that he could mark the target again. This time, his run in heading looked good. Seconds later, the rocket was fired and impacted right on target, the center of Hill 461. A cloud of white smoke rose up as the two jets came screaming out of the sky towards it.

Then, something completely unexpected happened; a red smoke grenade went off on the north side of the mountain no less than 50 meters from the impact of the Willie Pete rocket. The grunts had been taught that if they ever came under friendly fire, they were to pop a green smoke grenade which would signal their presence. Although this was a red smoke grenade, not green, I didn't want to take any chances and be responsible for bombing my own troops. There was always the chance that the man who popped the grenade simply didn't have a green one.

"Abort! Abort! Abort!" I yelled into the radio microphone.

There was a brief moment of dead silence on the radio, and I was about to scream "Abort" again.

"Roger, Alpha, what's going on down there? Do you have men on that hill, over?"

"Wait one. Skipper, we've got men on that hill, I can't bomb it!"

"Bullshit, Hunt. It's an enemy trick, bomb the hill!"

"Yes sir. Bulldozer X-ray, it was not our men. My six says it's an enemy trick and wants you to bomb the hill, over."

"Roger that, Alpha."

The AO circled once again setting himself up to make another pass at the mountain and marking the target with a

Willie Pete rocket. Moments later, white smoke rose from the Hill 461 again; and two jets descended upon their target.

Another red smoke grenade went off on the north side of the hill from the same spot as before. I could not do this. I could not bomb a hill that might have fellow Marines on it.

"Abort! Abort! Abort!" I screamed. Once again, the jets peeled off and rose back up into the sky.

"Alpha, are you sure you don't have men on that hill, over."

"Wait one, Bulldozer."

"Skipper, we must have men on that hill. I can't bomb it sir!"

"Damn it, Hunt, I said bomb the hill, our men are off the hill or dead."

The CO grabbed the microphone from my hand and keyed it.

"This is Alpha six. I said bomb the fucking hill!"

That was it, the CO would take full responsibility for this situation. I washed my hands of the matter. He was the one who had ordered the aerial observer to bomb the hill; and if battalion ever asked me what had happened, I was willing to tell them the exact story. I felt that we should not bomb the hill under these circumstances. I had been in country for over six months now, and I had never encountered a situation where the enemy tried to trick us from bombing him. I felt that such an action was probably rare, if it happened at all.

This time, the jets struck with the ferocity I had become accustomed to. Four huge fireballs rose from Hill 461 as napalm was scattered across the hill. Then, four rapid and successive explosions went off as four 500 pound bombs impacted in the same violent manner.

The retreating platoon had returned to our position carrying their wounded. I called for a medivac chopper and got them out before darkness descended upon us. The jets disappeared into the twilight, and I felt a bit relieved that they had only run one pass on the hill. Still, I feared that if I was right, any men who had survived the NVA attack were probably dead for sure by now.

"Alpha one four, this is Bulldozer X-ray. We've got to call it a day, but I'll be back first thing in the morning. Stay safe, Alpha."

"Roger, Bulldozer. Thanks for your help, out."

It was quiet now, no shooting, no explosions, and still no radio contact with the platoon that had been ambushed on Hill 461. I found my old foxhole and cleaned it out preparing for the night. I didn't know if I could sleep tonight, but exhaustion took over. Before I knew it, I was awakened by the dawn and a call on my radio.

"Alpha one four, this is Bulldozer X-ray, over."

It was the crack of dawn, perhaps 5:00 a.m.; and already the aerial observer was on station.

"Bulldozer X-ray, this is Alpha one four, over."

"Morning, Alpha. I'm enroute to your position and will be there in about five minutes. I want to check out that hill again."

"Roger Bulldozer, I'll be waiting, out."

Moments later, the familiar sound of the OV-10 Bronco broke the silence of the morning. The AO swooped downward and buzzed Hill 461. There was no enemy fire, which surprised me. "Had the NVA slipped away once again?" I wondered.

"Alpha, are you sure you don't have any men alive on that hill, over?"

"Not that I know of Bulldozer. My six said we left a few KIA there, but no one alive was left on the hill.

"Well I've got two men in a bomb crater, alive. One is waving a white T-shirt. I'm going in for a closer look."

The Bronco banked as it circled back to the north and then descended upon Hill 461 as it leveled its wings.

"Alpha, you've got men on that hill, alive; and they look to be burnt from napalm. One has blonde hair. Those are definitely friendlies. I'm calling for a medivac."

Well, there it was. The CO had bombed our own men. He wouldn't listen to me when we circled the hill and I saw a man jump into a foxhole. He wouldn't listen to me when I aborted the mission and told him that I thought we had men still alive on the hill. It would be on his conscience, not mine. He had ordered the bombing of his own men. I felt sick at the thought of it.

The AO continued to circle the hill and make low level passes to see if he drew any enemy fire; but he didn't. A CH-46 soon arrived on station, and I listened to the radio as the AO instructed the chopper pilot on where to land. The hill had been bombed so many times now that there were no trees left to obstruct the landing. But the hill was steep and the chopper could only set his tail wheels down as they so often had to do.

As the chopper approached the hill, Bulldozer X-ray continued to buzz the hill, ready to provide support and fire power if needed. That was the great thing about the OV-10 Bronco. It carried 20 millimeter rockets and six M-60 machine guns for ground support situations such as this. As the chopper set its wheels down, I looked out in anticipation of a sudden attack. Nothing would please the NVA more than to spring a trap and shoot down a helicopter, but nothing happened.

The tailgate came down, and the door gunners ran out the back to help the two wounded men board the chopper. I could only guess, but I suspected that they were asking the Marines if there were any other survivors. Apparently, there weren't. Moments later the helicopter lifted off and headed back to Dong Ha, where the men would receive medical treatment.

"Alpha, this is Bulldozer. There aren't any more known survivors according to your men. You'll want to tell your six what's going on and get some men up there to recover the KIA's. I'll remain on station a while longer in case you need me."

"Roger that, Bulldozer, and thanks for your help, out."

I made my way over to the CO and briefed him on the situation. Of course, I couldn't say anything to him about having bombed his own men, it wasn't my place to do so. I was sure that it wouldn't take long for the grunts to pass the scuttlebutt back to battalion. Everyone was ordered to pack up. We would be moving out soon to Hill 461.

At the end of that day, we were occupying Hill 461; and there was no sign of the enemy. I called in several choppers to recover the dead Marines that once made up first platoon. I couldn't help reflecting about all that had just happened. Twice now, we had been to this same piece of dirt they called Hill 461; and twice, we had been ambushed and had lost men. It seemed so senseless to keep fighting for the same piece of ground.

Before the day had ended, Alpha Company was helo lifted off of LZ Sierra and flown back to the FSB which was now called LZ Mac. Alpha Company would provide perimeter guard on LZ Mac. I learned that we had lost 7 men from the ambush and sustained 23 wounded. On November 21$^{st}$, we were once again helo lifted off of LZ Mac and flown to a small outpost in the flatlands called C-1. We had received new orders and would be working with an ARVN unit (Army of the Republic of Vietnam) in what was called "Pacification."

Our job would be to provide support for the ARVNS, while they rounded up people in the villages to check identity papers and weed out Viet Cong and draft dodgers. It sounded like easy duty for a change. At least, we were out of the mountains and back in the flatlands again.

*Bulldozer X-ray with his OV-10 Bronco*

# CHAPTER

# *FOURTEEN*

## PACIFICATION

From November 21st to December 9th, our battalion participated in a special program called "Pacification." This was probably the easiest operation I had encountered since landing in Vietnam. Basically, we surrounded numerous villages east of Route 1, while the 2nd ARVN Regiment rounded up all of the villagers, checked identity papers, and interrogated them to identify Viet Cong sympathizers and draft dodgers. The operation resulted in the arrest of 103 suspected VC and 60 draft dodgers.

On December 7th, Alpha Company was moved to a blocking position while the ARVN's swept through a village. We were in a clearing, and there was very little cover available. The area looked as though it had been cleared by bulldozers, because the trees were piled up on one side in heaps. Suddenly, we began taking incoming, 82 millimeter mortars.

I took cover immediately behind a pile of debris as the mortars began exploding all around us.

"One four man up! One four man up!" someone yelled.

The mortars were still exploding all around us, but someone was calling for me. I knew the drill; I left the cover of the tree pile and ran towards the voice.

"One four man up!"

"I'm here, I'm here!" I yelled as I ran towards the corpsman who was calling for me. Next to him was a wounded Marine he was trying to treat. As I stopped and dropped to my knees, another round impacted about 50 meters from us.

The doc was trying to stop the bleeding from the young Marine's head wound; but when I saw how bad, he was wounded, I knew it was just a matter of minutes before the grunt would be dead. A large chunk of his head was blown away; memories of Bach came back to my mind. Bach had died the same way – massive head wound from flying shrapnel. Within minutes, the man was pronounced dead. Only a routine medivac chopper would be needed this time.

The shelling soon stopped, and our artillery FO got a fix on the area where the tube was located – a village we had not yet visited. We couldn't fire on the mortar tube because it was coming from a friendly village, and we might kill or wound innocent South Vietnamese civilians. That's what this operation was all about, weeding out the Viet Cong that lived and operated among the innocent villagers. The CO sent a platoon ahead to investigate.

We moved out following what appeared to be a fire trail. It was a wide path that had been cleared by heavy equipment winding through an area of forests. By day's end, we were setting up a perimeter in a dry rice paddy. I went right to work digging a foxhole.

Suddenly, I realized that the mosquitoes were biting the hell out of me. It was breeding season for them, and most of the rice paddies were full of water. This was actually the first time I had taken notice of them. The biting was intense, and they were buzzing in my ears and all around my face. I rolled the sleeves of my fatigues down to protect my arms, but my face was completely exposed.

By nightfall, I could take no more. The only recourse I had was to put my poncho over my head to keep from getting bit. A poncho is made of rubber; although it kept the mosquitoes away from me, it raised the temperature and made sleeping almost impossible. My choices were to continue to be eaten alive by the mosquitoes, or endure the heat by wrapping my upper body inside the poncho. That seemed like the longest night I had spent in Vietnam. Fortunately, we moved away from this area the next morning and took up a position later that day in a very sandy area closer to the Gulf of Tonkin shore.

We spent several days in this village as the ARVN's continued to do their job. It was during this time that I began to become closer friends with the battalion one four man, Randy Williams. Randy was from Illinois. I had met him many months earlier when I first arrived in Vietnam, but our paths didn't seem to cross often. When I was in Alpha Company, he was in H & S Company. When I was transferred to H & S Company, he was transferred to Alpha. We had talked to each other often on the radio but had not been in the same company until now. I had been transferred back to H & S Company as a new one four man came into the unit and took my place in Alpha Company.

Randy and I built our tent together using our ponchos. By snapping them together, you could create a large tent that two men could sleep in. All that was needed was some wooden sticks to hold the two center ends up and some stakes to stretch out the sides.

The days were easy for us since there was little need for any air support during this part of the operation. Randy had a tape recorder, and we took turns recording tapes to send home to our families. He had also purchased a dagger with a leg sheath, and we took turns taking pictures of each other wearing the dagger on our legs. Randy had gotten a package from home with a box of cookies in it – that just made my day. Considering all that I had been through, these few days were terrific.

*Randy Williams*

Randy and I spent the days talking the same way Terry and I had done months earlier. The thought of what happened to Terry was always in the back of my mind, though; and I had reservations about getting to know Randy too well only to see something happen to him later on. So far it seemed that every man I became close to ended up dead. You needed to have friends just to stay sane so you could talk about the one thing that meant more to you than anything else – getting back to the world. As I've said before, it was conversations about home and things you used to do back in the world that motivated you to do whatever it took to survive. Without them, the days were even more difficult to bear.

Like all good things in Vietnam, those relaxing days came to an end on December 10$^{th}$. The entire battalion returned to Quang Tri to prepare for a new operation in the south. We would fly from Quang Tri to Da Nang on C-130's. From Da Nang, we would be moved by trucks to An Hoa. Because the Third Marine Regiment had been the innovators in building mountaintop landing zones and fire support bases, we would take our experience to an area called "Antennae Valley." Intelligence reports showed that enemy infiltration through this mountainous area, which bordered Laos, was on the increase.

This time, we would be operating under the command of First Marine Division. The operation would last several months, and enemy contact was expected. The good news was that when this operation ended, I would be what the short-timers called, "a two digit midget" – I would have less than 100 days left on my tour of duty in Vietnam.

As the trucks unloaded us at our rear headquarters in Quang Tri, I gazed across the landscape. The canvas tents had been replaced with plywood and sheet metal structures with wooden floors. The dirt road I had hitchhiked on several times before was now a paved, asphalt road. They had even built a small PX that sold some of the many comforts of home such as real soap, deodorant, tooth paste and shaving lotion. I also looked forward to more of that ice cold milk at the messhall.

That afternoon, I went by the supply tent to draw more ammo for my 45 pistol and some smoke grenades and new batteries for my radio. There, in the corner of the tent, stood a small, white Christmas tree with shiny glass balls hanging from its limbs. It was hard to believe that it would soon be Christmas. Having grown up in Norfolk, Virginia, we often had very cold weather and even snow at this time of the year. One year, my mother even put up a white Christmas tree similar to this one. The sight of this tree brought back such memories of home that I almost broke into tears. Vietnam was a long ways from home and any snow or cold weather. I wondered if I would ever see those things again. I asked the supply sergeant to snap a picture of me next to the tree.

*Weeks before Christmas – Quang Tri, 1968*

# CHAPTER

# *FIFTEEN*

## ANTENNAE ALLEY

On December 13, 1968, we landed at the An Hoa airfield east of Da Nang. We were to participate in an operation called Taylor/Common. Since my arrival in country I had participated in eight operations – Napoleon/Saline, Scotland, Kentucky, Lancaster II, Jones Creek, Scotland II, Lancaster II Jupiter, and Lancaster. The names were meaningless to me. Every day spent in Vietnam was a nightmare, and any day could be my last day on earth. I had been in Vietnam nearly eight months, yet the four months left on my tour seemed to stretch far into the future. The end of my tour seemed as far away as home itself. I wondered what lasting memories this operation would bring.

As I stepped off of the tailgate of the C-130, I could see mountains to the west, "Indian country." Intelligence reports estimated that over 3,000 NVA were operating in that region.

It had become a major infiltration point for this part of Vietnam. Our job would be to first establish a fire support base on a mountaintop called Hill 558. We had just two weeks to secure the hill and get the gun emplacements up and running so that a 155 millimeter artillery battery could provide support for us as we moved further west.

The area we were going into had been given the nickname "Antennae Alley." It was given this name because the area was dotted with steep, tall mountaintops, which stuck up from the landscape like dozens of antennae sticking up from houses across a suburban neighborhood. It made Mutter's Ridge look like a small hill. One mountaintop on which we would establish a landing zone was over 1000 meters high – more than twice as tall as Hill 461, where we had been ambushed twice.

We spent the night at An Hoa and departed the next day on CH-46 helicopters. I was still in the battalion CP, so at least I did not need to worry about going in on the first chopper this time. Bravo and Charlie Company would be flown in first. The battalion CP would come in last, after the hill had been secured.

The lift went smoothly with no enemy contact. By day's end, I was setting up my tent for the night and digging another foxhole. For the next several days, the companies sent out patrols down the mountain to look for the enemy. Engineers were flown in to blow trees off the hill, so that a bulldozer could be lowered and used to dig the gunpits.

Each day, the engineers would set dozens and dozens of sticks of C-4 around trees and then set them off. Prior to detonation, an engineer would yell out, "Fire in the hole!" Those words would be repeated down the hill and around the perimeter several times so that everyone could prepare for the detonation. We were instructed to get into our foxholes because the explosion would send all kinds of debris from the shattered trees into the air.

"Fire in the hole!"

I sat in the bottom of my foxhole with my fingers in my ears to help stifle the loud explosion that would soon follow. Seconds later, a horrendous boom echoed across the mountaintop and splinters and dirt rained down on us.

"Corpsman up! Corpsman up!"

"Great, someone evidently didn't follow instructions, and someone got injured," I muttered to myself.

The "all clear" signal was given, and we all started crawling out of our foxholes curious to know what had happened and who needed the corpsman.

Twenty or thirty meters away, I saw a group of men huddled together in a circle, evidently looking at the injured man. I walked over to see what was going on. It was Maxwell. Lance Corporal Maxwell was one of the battalion radio operators.

Just when I thought I had seen every conceivable way for a man to get injured or killed, something new in pain and suffering reared its ugly face. The explosion had lifted a large boulder weighing hundreds of pounds from the top of the hill, hurling it down to our position. The boulder struck Maxwell square on top of his head, breaking his neck and pushing his skull down upon his shoulders. The corpsman was trying to insert a tube down his throat to clear his air passage, but within minutes he was dead. Who could have even imagined that such a thing could happen? The boulder could have hit any one of us. I guessed Maxwell would be classified as "killed by friendly fire."

After the FSB was finished and the guns were brought in, the word came down that the hill would be called "FSB Maxwell" in honor of the man who gave his life for this base to be built.

In the days to come, our patrols found numerous small camps with straw huts and bunkers as well as caches of weapons, rice and other supplies. There was plenty of evidence of enemy activity in the area, but no major fighting occurred. A few VC were spotted and killed. One night, our lines were probed by a few of them; but, basically, the time we spent on FSB Maxwell was uneventful.

*Antennae Valley seen from FSB Maxwell*

Most of us put the unfortunate death of Lance Corporal Maxwell behind us as we turned our thoughts to the Christmas holiday rapidly approaching.

On Christmas day, I attended a mass held by the battalion chaplain. A delicious hot meal was flown out to us that included turkey and gravy, mashed potatoes, green beans, sweet potatoes, and cranberry sauce. We even had semi-cold coca-cola and pumpkin pie for dessert. New Years was just a week away, which meant that I only had four months to go before leaving. Now, more than ever, my thoughts focused completely on surviving and what I would do when I returned home.

I had been sending almost every paycheck I earned home to my parents towards my plan to purchase a new 1969 Mustang Mach I. I had picked out the color and features – candy apple red with white interior, a 390 cubic inch engine, four on the floor, and an eight track tape player. A new sports car was what most of us dreamed of buying when we got back home. With combat pay, I was sending $235.00 a month home; but it would still not be enough to pay cash for the car. It was hard to believe that I was risking my life every day for a year for such a small amount of money.

New Years came without incident, and I celebrated my 21st birthday on January 2nd. I managed to save a can of peaches and a can of pound cake which served as my birthday cake – no candles though.

Charlie Company vacated FSB Maxwell and flew west to set up another LZ. The battalion CP accompanied them. This new hill was extremely steep, and it was difficult to make a flat area to sleep on. When mornings came, the clouds were below us covering the valley like a blanket of cotton. We took a few rounds of mortars one day, but the mountain was so steep that most impacted below the summit where the LZ was located.

We moved again to another mountaintop, and this one was much broader and had a nice flat area for landing a helicopter. As we were setting up our CP, I came upon an NVA bunker and decided to check it out. Inside I found a Chinese SKS, a rifle similar to the Russian AK-47. Wow! What a find! I had captured my first enemy weapon, which I desperately wanted to keep and take home with me.

You were allowed to take such weapons home, but only after the firing pin had been removed. I kept the weapon close by but knew that it was added weight to carry. Eventually, I tagged it with my name and sent it back to the rear to be stored in Quang Tri. I should have known that I would never see the rifle again.

*Chinese SKS Rifle Captured*

On January 15<sup>th</sup>, I was handling the LZ as a chopper called to inform me that he was inbound to my position. One of our platoons had encountered some sniper fire on the north side of the LZ just minutes earlier. I called the chopper pilot on my radio.

"Big Boy Zulu, this is Bus Stop one four, over."

"Ah roger, Bus Stop, approaching your AO. Pop smoke, over."

"Negative, Big Boy. I'm flashing mirror at your ten o'clock. Approach from the south, and leave from the south. We've been taking sniper fire from the north, over."

"Ah roger, understand. I have Hallmark on board to see your six. Is it safe to remain in your LZ, over?"

"Roger, Big Boy; but be sure to come and leave from the south, over."

"Roger that, out."

The chopper was a Huey Gunship. He was carrying the regimental commander as well as several other high ranking officers including the sergeant major of the Marine Corps. They were coming to talk with our battalion commander, and the chopper wanted to shut down and wait for his valuable passengers rather than waste fuel circling overhead. Having a helicopter land and stay in your LZ was risky, since it could invite incoming; but, so far, this operation had been without major contact with the enemy. Several choppers had landed on FSB Maxwell and stayed for 30 minutes or more.

The Huey landed without incident coming in from the south, as I had instructed. A half hour later his passengers boarded, and he started his engines preparing to leave. Just as he lifted off, he turned and headed north, even though I had told him to come and leave from the south.

Pop! Pop! Pop! Three AK-47 rounds were fired and the chopper exploded in a ball of fire less than 100 meters from the LZ. It plummeted down the mountain almost instantly. The sniper had just taken down the chopper that was carrying some of the top brass of this operation. Eight men were now dead counting the pilot, co-pilot and two door gunners. Later that day I was questioned by our colonel as to what exactly had happened. I told him that I had instructed the pilot to come in and leave from the south and he acknowledged that request. But when he left he ignored my instructions and flew out to the north, right over the area from which the sniper fire had come. Perhaps the pilot had simply forgotten the instructions I had given him – but what a costly error!

Days later, we were helo lifted off of this mountaintop and moved further west to another mountain, where we would provide support for engineers to build another FSB. It was during this time that I began to feel sick.

First I developed a fever; and my body ached all over. I thought it was a cold or maybe the flu; but within 24 hours, I felt much worse than any cold had ever made me feel. The corpsman checked my temperature – 105 degrees. I had contracted malaria. I radioed for my own medivac.

I was medivaced to a hospital in Da Nang. I had a daily temperature of 105 degrees, and they took blood from me every hour for the first 24 hours. I had to stand in a cold shower for 30 minutes in an effort to bring my fever down. I was in the shower for 30 minutes, then out for 30 minutes, then in again. I was shivering and freezing. During the 30 minutes I was out of the shower, they draped cold alcohol towels over my body and had a fan blowing on me to try to bring my temperature down.

They took urine samples, stool samples, blood samples; but they didn't treat me with any medications. The doctors couldn't treat me until they knew what strain of malaria I had. This went on for two days, and I was nearly delirious from the fever and the chills. It was the sickest I had ever been, and I just wanted to die.

Finally, on the third day, the doctor started giving me shots and said that I had the worst strain of malaria there was. However, the good news was that I was less likely to have a relapse later in life. (Malaria stays in your blood for the rest of your life; therefore, you cannot donate blood to anyone.)

Slowly the temperature subsided, and I began to get well. I remained in the hospital for two weeks. When I was released, I was given two more weeks of light duty which meant that I could not go to the field. I flew back to Quang Tri on a C-130 and did not see the battalion again until the Antennae Valley operation was over.

I had less than 100 days left in Vietnam. I relished in the thought of finally becoming a two digit midget. I wanted to do something to count down my final days in the Nam. During my short stay in the battalion rear at Quang Tri, I bought a Playboy magazine at the PX. I removed the centerfold and drew a bikini across her top and bottom. I then broke the bikini down into squares so that I could color each square in, one at a time, as each remaining day ended. By the time I left Vietnam, my centerfold would no longer be nude. Now, all I had to do was survive those final three months.

# CHAPTER

# *SIXTEEN*

## INTO THE A SHAU VALLEY

The battalion returned from its operation in the Antennae Valley region on February 21st. It then moved by truck to Vandergrift Combat Base, where the companies provided perimeter guard for the base running daily, routine patrols. It was a fairly uneventful period, and I was getting "shorter" every day that passed. I was beginning to feel more confident that I just might survive the war and looked forward to my return to civilization, when another bizarre incident occurred.

I had recently made a new friend, Bill Walls. I met Bill months earlier when he first arrived in Vietnam. He was a radio operator also, and they placed him in H & S Company. Bill and I became friends right away because he was from Virginia Beach, and I was from Norfolk. He actually gave me the name and address of his ex-girlfriend, Linda Woods from Virginia Beach. I had been writing to her since then, and we had been making plans to meet once I returned home.

On March 15th, Bill had tried to get me to go with him to chow; but my experience of ten months told me that if you're getting short, you don't want to be caught in a large group. There was a common saying, "one round will get you all." So I passed on the invitation and told him I'd rather wait until the line went down. Besides, I had a new letter to read.

When the familiar word came down that a one four man was needed to call in a medivac, I grabbed my radio but was stopped by Randy Williams (who was also with H & S Company at the time). "I've got this one, finish reading your letter man."

A group of grunts fresh back from patrol were waiting in the chow line at the mess hall. Some of the men started pushing and shoving, just horsing around. One of the men had a "bouncing betty" grenade tied to his flak jacket. The grenade was tied by the ring that is connected to the firing pin.

The "bouncing betty" got its name from the fact that, when it went off, it would first bounce upwards propelled by a small charge. A split second later, it would explode, generally at a height of about four to five feet. Exploding at that height insured instant death to anyone standing close by.

The pushing and shoving became reckless, and then it happened – the grenade fell off, armed, and exploded seconds later. Two men were killed instantly; three were seriously wounded; and seventeen others were slightly wounded. One of them was Bill Walls. The explosion not only wounded him from the flying shrapnel, but also perforated his ear drum rendering him permanently deaf in one ear. I suddenly realized that my experience had probably just saved my life.

We received new orders for an operation into the A Shau Valley, which was notorious for being the primary infiltration route for the NVA. They called the route, which entered from Laos, the "Ho Chi Minh Trail." I had heard so many stories about the A Shau Valley that it was enough to scare the hell out of anyone, especially someone getting "short" as I was.

A buddy of mine said that 9th Marines had just been pulled out of the valley "and got the shit kicked out of 'em." He said that a recon squad had been sent in a few days ago to check out the situation where we would be landing. The squad took pictures of the road as they walked down it. When they returned, the pictures were developed and showed NVA hidden in the brush and trees, watching every move the squad made. They didn't attack because they didn't want to give away their position. The NVA knew that if a recon team came in, a larger unit would follow. They would be their target.

The helo lift would take place at night. I had never been on a night lift, nor had any other unit to my knowledge. I was disliking this operation more and more. This was not the kind of operation you wanted to go on when you had little more than a month left in country. To make matters worse, I was informed that I would be going back out to a line company – Charlie Company.

I had been through intense battles, incoming, malaria, losing friends; and now they were sending me back to a line company on an operation in an area more notorious than the DMZ. With less than 60 days to go, I just knew that the irony of this would be for me to get killed just before I was to go home.

On March 19th, we assembled on the runway to await the helicopters that would take us into the A Shau Valley. Fortunately, I was not going in on the first chopper. It was nearly dark when the choppers lifted off.

The chopper ride lasted much longer than I had anticipated. I was beginning to wonder just how far we had traveled, when the chopper descended and finally landed. The tailgate came down, and the 18 of us on board rushed out the back. I was in awe when I realized where we were. The chopper had landed at Quang Tri airbase. All of the choppers had landed here. They couldn't find the LZ in the dark so they aborted the mission – another typical example of that three-ring circus.

The next day, they lifted us in full daylight to the valley. The hill where the battalion headquarters was set up had over 50 bunkers on it and was believed to have been an NVA battalion headquarters. Each bunker could house and sleep 3 men.

Charlie Company was on a hill that overlooked the border between South Vietnam and Laos. Each day we could hear tracked vehicles moving somewhere on the Laos side. One evening a vehicle was spotted trying to cross a bridge near the border. I called in an airstrike which bombed the bridge and the vehicle, scoring a direct hit.

On March 30th, one of our platoons found a bunker complex near our position. I called for an aerial observer to keep an eye on the platoon and the area around them, as they searched the complex.

Each day, our companies were finding bunkers and huts throughout the area, with lots of signs of recent enemy activity. Small encounters with squad-size groups of NVA occurred, but no major battles. Airstrikes were run against some of the bunker complexes by the company one four men. Some companies took incoming mortars from time to time, as well as rockets that we could actually see being fired from Laos. I called an airstrike in on the rocket positions, but the AO said they had retreated into caves and the strikes proved to be ineffective.

On April 4th, Echo Company from 2nd Battalion, 3rd Marines was attacked by a large NVA force. Echo was operating with our battalion along the Ho Chi Minh trail when the attack came. Waves of NVA struck their lines firing RPG's, mortars, and automatic weapons; but Echo prevailed and defeated the attackers.

On April 6th, I received word that a replacement was coming to Charlie Company. I would be returned to the battalion CP where I would remain until the end of my tour. I was relieved to be getting out of the line company. Later that day, I was flown by chopper to the battalion CP, where I quickly found an abandoned NVA bunker and made it my new home.

The next day, I had to stand radio watch in the CP tent. I took out my entrenching tool and began digging a foxhole, while everyone around me looked at me like I was crazy. No one else had dug such a hole. No sooner had I finished than we began taking incoming artillery, 75 and 82 millimeter mortars. I jumped into my foxhole while everyone else just lay on the ground with no protection. When the barrage was over, everyone else started digging.

On April 7th, we took more incoming, 122 millimeter rockets. I called for an aerial observer, and he spotted a company-size force moving out from the area where we suspected the rockets had originated. He called in an airstrike of snake and nape, which caused several large secondary explosions. We had hit their supply of rockets.

We continued to take incoming nearly every day. The CP was located on a fire support base called FSM Sparks. A battery of 155 millimeter howitzers were the primary target. I thought it was rather dumb to put the battalion headquarters in a position that would surely draw enemy fire at every opportunity. I spent most of my time in my NVA bunker or next to my foxhole in the battalion CP tent standing radio watch.

Our companies continued to find caches of weapons and supplies and to engage small bands of NVA soldiers. On April 12th, one patrol encountered a small band of NVA. A white man with blonde hair and a blonde beard was seen with them; rumors floated that he was a Russian advisor.

On April 14th, the battalion was helo-lifted out of the area and flown farther east to another mountaintop. One evening, I was given the task to run a special bombing mission with an A-6 Intruder. I was now the senior one four man in the battalion, so I felt honored to be chosen for this special mission. A new device had been flown out to us – a small box with a red button on it. A PRC-47 radio was also flown out. This radio was a UHF radio which allowed me to talk directly to the jet.

The box transmitted a special radio signal to the jet which he could use to determine our precise location on the ground. Then, I was to give the pilot an azimuth from that position and a direction to a target I wanted bombed. This was a test mission to try out the new device. Our air liaison officer was with me to help out if needed.

"Bus Stop one four, this is Beefsteak Bravo, over."

"Beefsteak Bravo, this is Bus Stop one four, over."

"Ah roger, Bus Stop. I'm inbound with running lights on, over."

"Roger, Beefsteak. I have you in sight. Bombing mission, azimuth two one five, distance one thousand meters, over."

The A-6 pilot acknowledged the mission as he punched the numbers into his computer.

"Bus Stop one four, I'm ready for i-dent, over."

"Roger, Beefsteak. I-denting now, over." I pushed the red button on the box. Silently it sent out a signal to the pilot.

"Roger, Bus Stop. I-dent complete, over."

"Roger. What is your ordinance Beefsteak, over?"

"Five hundred pounders, over."

"Roger, drop four, over."

"Roger, Bus Stop. I'm gonna make a trial run first with lights on. Tell me how it looks, over."

The jet flew to the east of our mountaintop as expected, and the mission was a go.

"Roger, Beefsteak. Looks good. Go hot, over."

"Roger, Bus Stop. Understand go for hot. Turning lights out."

The jet quickly disappeared in the dark night sky, and all we could do was follow the sound of his engines. Seconds past as the jet circled our mountain.

It now sounded like the jet was heading straight at us instead of flying to our east as he did on the dummy run. The jet was being flown by its computer, not by the pilot. He could not see us, and we could not see him.

Closer and closer it came, when suddenly the air liaison officer grabbed the radio handset from me.

"Abort! Abort! Abort!" He yelled.

"Ooops, too late! Bombs away!"

Four 500 pound bombs were rapidly descending to earth, straight at us! I hit the ground and covered my head with my hands, as I listened to the swishing sound of the bombs coming down. For an instant, I thought for sure that this was the end. I was going to be killed just weeks before leaving and by my own people!

The bombs impacted on the side of our mountain scaring the hell out of everybody. The colonel came running out of his tent, "What the hell are you doing, Hunt? Trying to kill us all?"

That's just great, now I'm getting blamed for it all when all I did was push a button as I was told to do. The air liaison officer went over to talk to the colonel and explain what had happened. The jet turned and headed back to his base; and I headed back to my tent for the night, again wondering how I would ever survive this insanity.

Finally on April 19th, the battalion was lifted out of the A Shau Valley and sent back to Vandergrift Combat Base. The operation was over, and I now had 30 days left in country. It was doubtful I would see another operation. I had persevered. I had survived. I would not be going out to the field again.

CHAPTER

# *SEVENTEEN*

## WELCOME HOME

On May 19, 1969, I returned home from my year tour in Vietnam. It was a very long day. I first took a plane from Okinawa to Wake Island. From Wake Island, we flew to Hawaii and from Hawaii to San Francisco. Upon arrival in San Francisco, I immediately went to a restroom and changed out of my dress uniform, because I had heard tales that Vietnam Veterans were not being treated well and that the war was being blamed on them. Since I had turned 21 in Vietnam, I wanted to celebrate my birthday. I went to the bar and purchased my first legal alcoholic beverage (a bloody mary).

I caught a commercial airline to Chicago's O'Hare airport. From there, I changed planes and flew to New York and from New York to Newport News, Virginia. The last leg of my nearly 24 hour journey ended in Norfolk, Virginia where I landed at about 6:30 p.m.

*Waiting for the plane to take me home*

My parents and Linda Woods were there to greet me. I had ordered that candy apple red, 1969 Mustang Mach I months earlier; and my parents drove it to the airport to pick me up. You can imagine the joy I felt to finally be home from the war, driving my brand new sports car, and meeting Linda after months of letter exchanges.

*Linda, Bob and Mach I, May 20, 1969*

The joy of finally being home didn't last long. I was home on leave for several weeks before reporting to Quantico Marine Base, where I served the remaining months of my enlistment with a student training battalion. Our job was to train officer candidates. I spent most of my weekends on base because, we were on call frequently for riot control in Washington, DC – protests against the war.

While at Quantico, another bizarre incident occurred that brought back vivid memories of Vietnam. Looking back, I believe this incident was another trigger to my Post Traumatic Stress Disorder.

We were in the field demonstrating the use of air support when attacking an enemy position. A unit of female officer candidates was sitting in bleachers that looked out over the terrain where the demonstration was to occur. I was appointed to be the one four man and direct an airstrike on a position a thousand meters in front of us. The aircraft being used that day was a single engine propeller driven trainer. The plane didn't actually carry any ordinance. It was to be a simulated bomb drop.

As I was talking with the pilot, he turned his aircraft inverted heading straight for the target. He was showing off for the female officer candidates sitting in the bleachers.

"Yankee Zulu, you'd better roll back over. You can't drop a bomb upside down, over."

"Ah roger. "

The plane was no more than 100 meters high when it began to roll back over. Suddenly, the plane dove straight for the ground and exploded in a ball of fire just 500 meters from the bleachers. I was astounded. The pilot died instantly.

The demonstration was immediately ended, and later the Criminal Investigation Division questioned me asking what I had said to the pilot before he crashed his aircraft. This was the beginning of a new war for me – the war inside.

Just when I thought I was putting the war behind me, this had to happen. All of those memories of death and destruction were flooding my mind. I needed to get away from the military as quickly as possible. I needed to start a new life, the life of a civilian, and put the war behind me once and for all.

I was able to obtain a three-month cut from my enlistment so that I could start college at Old Dominion University in Norfolk. I had applied and been accepted in their engineering program and planned to attend on the GI Bill. Linda and I had a short "engagement" and eloped on June 28th in Elizabeth City, North Carolina, on a weekend I was free to leave the base. When we returned home to tell our parents, her mother said, "Couldn't you find anything better to do on a weekend?"

Linda worked for the telephone company as a secretary, so we had planned to live on her paycheck and my VA benefits. We rented a small one-bedroom apartment. To make ends meet, I ended up selling my beautiful Mustang not long after I got out of the Marines, so that we would have only one car payment. Linda owned a Volkswagen Beetle and would drive me to college on her way to work and pick me up afterwards.

I had been in college for a few weeks, when my English professor gave us an assignment. We were to write an essay about our summer vacations. Since I hadn't really had a vacation that summer, I struggled to find something worthwhile to write about.

My fellow classmates were writing stories about drunken beach parties, trips to the mountains with friends and families, and summer jobs. I decided to write about my final days in Vietnam. The war was behind me physically but still lingered strongly in my mind.

I wrote about the heat, the constant fear, death, destruction, the loss of friends, and the struggle to survive and get back home. I wrote about the anguish with which I was dealing. I wrote about the pride I had for having served my country and having been a United States Marine. I wrote the truth; and, although it wasn't a literary masterpiece, I felt it was a worthwhile topic.

When the professor handed the graded papers back to us, he made a point to ridicule and belittle me – my paper had a large red "D-" at the top.

"Now here's a young man who thought it wise to write about the war in Vietnam, as if anyone really cared to hear more about that. Not exactly a Pulitzer Prize winning paper, Mr. Hunt, D minus. You might want to rethink future writing assignments."

Everyone in the class was laughing at his remarks. It made me feel as though they were making fun of me and thought my service to my country was a complete joke. There would not be any future "writing assignments" for me.

In an instant, the pride I had felt for my service to my country was taken away from me. That moment changed my life as much as the war had changed it. I took the paper from his hand, gave him a dirty look, then turned and walked out of his classroom. I quickly strode over to the dean's office and withdrew from college.

For some reason, that one single incident hurt more than everything I had endured in Vietnam. It seemed to me that no one cared that men were fighting a war to protect our country, dying, and enduring horrible atrocities. People were demonstrating against the war in Washington, they were spitting at Vietnam Veterans, blaming the war on them. This insult in the classroom was the last straw for me. I vowed that day that I would never talk about the war again. I would never share my experiences. I would not even acknowledge that I had fought in the war. I would put the war behind me and forget about it.

Of course, quitting school did not sit well with my new, young wife. I was now faced with the reality of having to find a job that would provide for advancement and a future. I had no skills, no experience in the workforce other than a summer job in construction; and I did not want to be a construction worker.

I went to a personnel agency in hopes that they could place me in some sort of management training program. The agency was able to set up an interview with Household Finance Corporation. At the time, I didn't even own a suit. When I attended the interview, I wore a plain pair of slacks and shirt without a necktie and sandals without socks. I was completely out of place and out of my league. I'd never even been on a job interview before, so I didn't know what to expect or how to act.

I was given a number of tests and scored well. The interview must have gone well, because the next day I received a telephone call offering me a job as a manager trainee. The caller advised me to wear a suit WITH socks when I reported to work the following week.

It didn't take long before I fell into a routine in my new job. First, I learned how to take a credit application, how to process that application and how to make the credit decision. After six months of this aspect of the training, I was taught how to collect the loans that were made. It was this aspect of the job that actually gave me the most enjoyment.

I felt that, as a bill collector, I had a form of control over people. My attitude became one of revenge – revenge for the way I had been treated after my return from the war, revenge for the men whom I had seen die, revenge for the year of my life I had missed, and revenge for the lack of concern for the anguish I was holding inside of me. I took pleasure in repossessing furniture, television sets, and other items our company financed.

I demanded money from people who didn't have the money, even though they had legally contracted to pay it back. I was hated by some customers and was even threatened by a few. That just made me feel "cocky," and I would tell them to "take a number and get in line."

One day, I had just returned from two weeks' vacation during which I had decided to grow a mustache. It was now showing well but had not reached maturity. When I entered the office, my manager took one look at me and made the comment that my upper lip "looked like a hen's ass." Well, I just blew up. I swore at him and told him I quit. I was not going to let anyone treat me with such disrespect when I had fought for my country, even shed blood for my country. I threw a coat hanger at him and walked out of the office.

For seven years, I jumped from job to job, never really able to find whatever it was that I was searching for. I worked for Borg Warner Acceptance Corporation as a collection manager. I rented a U-haul truck at the end of every month and went out to repossess furniture the company had financed. My motto was "pay up or give up the sticks." The office was running with 30% delinquency when they hired me; and when I quit a year later, I had brought the delinquency down to 3%.

I took a job with a company called Home Mortgage as a mortgage broker. That job bored me because I had to be nice to people. All I did was take mortgage credit applications. Eventually, I was transferred to Richmond, Virginia and made manager of my own office; but I didn't want to be a manager.

So I quit that job and went to work for the Bank of Virginia as a credit officer. It looked like I was out of the bill collecting business for good. I was put in charge of their authorization department. It was my job to examine accounts for credit line increases and to handle authorizations on Master Charge accounts, when a charge would take the customer over his credit limit.

I had 38 women working under me, and how I ever got put in such a position was a complete mystery to me. I hated managing people and never really wanted to do that for a living. I was great at making credit decisions and collecting past due accounts, but I was lousy at managing. I had very poor people skills because of the anger I still carried inside of me.

I had been home from the war for seven years now, but inside the war was still a major part of my day-to-day life. I was searching for answers but could find none. I felt lost, empty, misunderstood. I needed help but didn't realize it. I had Post Traumatic Stress Disorder but had never heard of it. I was a psychological mess, and I knew that something had to change soon.

My outbursts continued to come without warning. One evening my wife and I were walking through a shopping mall. There was a soft serve ice cream stand, and I felt like having an ice cream. I ordered a large cone of chocolate. When the young teenage girl handed me what I felt was less than a large size, I got mad, turned the cone over and smashed it onto the counter, muttering an obscenity at her as I turned and walked away without paying.

Basically, I had turned bitter towards everyone, cynical, hateful. The war had ended for me, but a new war had been brewing inside of me for seven years. I took my anger and frustration out on anyone who got in my way or gave me trouble. I was heading for an all time low in my life.

# CHAPTER

# *EIGHTEEN*

## THE WAR INSIDE

Seven years had passed since I returned home from the war, yet I was still living it each and every day. A few months after my return, I began having horrific nightmares. The nightmares would wake me up, screaming and drenched in a cold sweat. Each nightmare was similar and vivid. I would dream that I was back in Vietnam and we were taking incoming. It was exploding all around me, and then I could see an artillery round coming straight at me. If I didn't wake myself up, it would explode and kill me.

These nightmares continued for those seven years during which I tried to cope with civilian life. I had not talked to anyone about the war or my experiences since that day in college, when I was ridiculed and belittled. I had not even told my wife what I had been through. I had kept it bottled up inside for all those years, and I was reaching a point of self-destruction. I had no friends. I had no one to talk to who could relate to what I had been through and what I was going through now. I was not doing well at my job either, and some employees had complained about me to management. I felt like I was boxed into a corner, and my day-to-day life was becoming the same as my nightmares. If I didn't break out of this cycle, I would die.

The memories of every event that had happened to me were as clear in my mind as if they had happened just yesterday. The loss of Terry, of Bach, and Lieutenant Wiley when his arm had been blown off kept haunting at me. The questions I struggled with day in and day out were "Why me? Why did I survive and they didn't? Why was my wound superficial when Lieutenant Wiley, a pilot with a future in aviation, lost his arm and possibly his future?"

I had two beautiful daughters now, Jennifer, age 4-1/2 and Melissa, age 18 months. We were doing well financially, and no one would think that anything was wrong. I never complained. I never showed the anguish openly. I just tried to deal with it the best I could.

One day, I came home from work and it was pouring down rain. When I pulled up in front of my apartment, I found that my assigned parking space was taken. An older woman lived in the apartment across the street from ours, and she had several teenage sons who drove cars. One of her sons had taken my parking space, and this wasn't the first time it had happened. But on that day, I decided that enough was enough. I parked behind the car in my space, blocking him in. I got out and walked over to her apartment and banged loudly on the door. When she came to the door, I said, "Get your damn car out of my parking space, or I'll have it towed away."

"You can't talk to me that way. We can park anywhere we want to," she argued.

"I said move the damn car, lady, NOW!"

"I'm calling the police!"

"Call the fucking police, but move that damn car now!"

I was furious, ready to explode. I got back in my car and just drove around for an hour or so. When I returned, the car was gone, and I parked in my own space.

The next day, Linda called me at work. She said the police had come to arrest me for curse and abuse. I left work early and went down to the police station to turn myself in. They arrested me on a misdemeanor charge and released me on my own recognizance.

A week later I went to court. The lady repeated her story to the judge, and the judge asked me if I had cursed at her. "You're damn right I did, your honor."

"Guilty as charged," he said. I paid the $10.00 fine and went home.

A few days later in September 1976, I went to work as I had done every day; but I had formulated a plan. That afternoon I walked into my boss's office and handed him my resignation. I packed up my personal belongings and went home.

During my lunch hour that day, I had paid a visit to the local Army Recruiting Office. I had joined the Army. (I actually tried to join the Marines again, but they wouldn't take me back saying that once you get out you can't come back in.) I just wanted to get back among men I could talk to, men who had experienced the war and who could relate to the things I had been through.

When I arrived home from work earlier than usual, I explained to my wife what I had done. To say the least, it was difficult for her to understand how I could throw away such a good job and go back into the military. But she stuck by me.

When I entered the Army, I was first sent to Fort Leonard Wood, Missouri for a three-week refresher course. Unlike at boot camp, I had freedom to come and go as I pleased when we weren't in classes or at a weapons range. The course was called Minute Man Training and was for men who had prior military service. We had to requalify on the use of the M-16 rifle, and we had to fire some of the other standard weapons at various rifle ranges. It was easy duty.

What amazed me was that every man in my class was a Vietnam Veteran. Every man had similar stories to tell, and most were re-entering military service for the same reason as I – they couldn't cope with civilian life.

After completing Minute Man Training, I was sent to Fort Sill, Oklahoma for a six-week course in Field Artillery Survey. I had been given a choice in jobs, at least to some degree. I chose this MOS because I felt that perhaps, if I didn't make the military a career, I could at least get a job as a surveyor afterwards.

I had lost most of my rank when I entered the Army, going from a Corporal (E-4) to a Private First Class (E-2), but after completing my survey training, I had advanced back to my prior equivalent rank, Specialist Four (E-4). My new orders after graduation sent me to Fort Bragg, North Carolina. I had signed up to go there but was supposed to be assigned to the 18th Corp Artillery. Instead they assigned me to the 82nd Airborne, which required that I attend jump school at Fort Benning, Georgia.

My wife and children joined me at Fort Bragg and for the first time in seven years, I felt like I was doing something I was meant to do. I felt a part of something bigger than myself. I felt like I fit in once again; but when I flew down to Fort Benning, my attitude returned briefly.

I was 28 years old now and was suddenly being treated the same as I was when I went through boot camp at Parris Island. I was ordered to get down and do pushups, and that did not sit well with me. I refused, and then I quit jump school. I had only been there two days.

When I returned to Fort Bragg, I was soon transferred again. This time they sent me to Fort Stewart, Georgia. I had learned a few things now that I had been back in the military for about a year. One thing I had learned was that the battalion armorer never went to the field. As a field artillery surveyor, I had to go to the field often and that meant spending time away from my family. I hated it. So when I arrived at Fort Stewart, I lied and told my new First Sergeant that I had been the battalion armorer at my previous unit. "Battalion Armorer" was not an MOS. It was more of a "hey you" detail assigned to anyone the battalion felt they could do without for a few months. It was more like punishment than anything else, but I didn't care as long as it got me out of the field.

I knew nothing about being an armorer, but I did know how to take a weapon apart quickly and put it back together. They made me the battalion armorer, and I quickly learned the job. By the time I had gotten new orders for Germany, the battalion had endured an inspection by the Inspector General (IG) and the armory passed with "no gigs noted." My reward was a promotion to Sergeant (E-5).

The nightmares had subsided now, coming only about once every six months. They weren't as intense either. I felt good. I was advancing in my new career. Because I was older than most of the men in my unit, many of the younger men looked up to me and often asked what it was like to be in combat. I was talking freely about the war and my experiences now, and my attitude had changed dramatically. I was finally starting to put the war behind me.

I transferred to Germany for a three-year tour, and it went well. I got promoted again to Staff Sergeant (E-6) and received an Army Commendation Medal for serving in the battalion mail room and passing another IG inspection with "no gigs noted." This time they sent me back to Fort Sill.

My four-year enlistment was up, and I decided to stay in the Army for another four years. I was given my choice of duty stations for reenlisting, so I chose to go back to Germany. My wife and I had enjoyed the previous tour, and I thought it would be great to get back there.

However, this second tour turned out far differently than the first one. Linda and I had grown apart over the years, and I'm not exactly sure why. The kids were getting older now, and both were attending grade school. This left little for her to do during the day, so she took an office job at the base. It was during this time that she met another man. When I found out about it from one of the kids, I was floored. How could this have happened? Again I found myself searching for answers and finding none.

After 14 years of marriage our lives were suddenly in turmoil. One day my commander told me not to go home, that my wife was moving out. Weeks later she left on a plane, and I assumed custody of our two children, Jennifer and Melissa.

My attitude slid, and I became depressed. I had two small children to take care of, and that made it difficult to deal with the day-to-day duties of the Army. I was thousands of miles from my home. I felt alone again, lost, searching for answers.

I approached my commander, and in strict confidence, asked if there was a way to get out of the Army under an honorable discharge. There was a way out. Under Army regulations, if my commander barred me from reenlistment, I could request to be discharged honorably. I asked the commander to bar me, and he did. The papers said that I could not deploy "combat ready" because I had two small children to care for. On February 8, 1984, we returned from Germany, and I was honorably discharged from the Army. I was a civilian once again.

CHAPTER

# *NINETEEN*

## COMING FULL CIRCLE

After I had been discharged from the Army, my daughters and I went to stay with my parents until I could find a job and get back on my feet again. I only had a few hundred dollars to my name and had to rent a car until my vehicle arrived by ship from Germany.

I had been home one day and went out to look for a job. The kids stayed with my mother. On my way home, I passed a Krispy Kreme Doughnut store and the "hot doughnuts" sign was turned on. I stopped and purchased a dozen hot doughnuts – a real treat for someone who had been out of the United States for two years, living in a foreign country with different customs and different eating habits.

It was only ten o'clock in the morning when I walked into the house and offered the kids a fresh doughnut. My mother went ballistic, and her anger brought back all of those memories from long ago.

"They're not eating doughnuts, it will ruin their lunch!" she yelled.

"A doughnut isn't going to ruin their lunch, Mom." I tried to explain.

"As long as you're living in my house, you'll do as I say. I'm the mother, and you're the son."

"And they're my kids, not yours; and if I want to give them a doughnut, I will."

"Get out! Get out of my house now!"

She ran to the bedroom, pulled open the dresser drawers and started grabbing piles of the kids clothes in her arms. Then, she ran to the front door, opened it and threw the clothes out into the yard.

"Get out, damn you! Get out of my house now!"

The kids were crying and I was in shock. My step-father just stood there and said nothing, did nothing. So I gathered all of our belongings together, put the kids in the rental car as quickly as I could, and drove away.

I felt as though I had come full circle now. I left home fourteen years ago because of my mother and her mental illnesses. Now it was all happening again, but this time she had directed her anger at my children. (This was the first of many incidents where my children were exposed to her abuse.)

We drove to a local mall, and I began thumbing through the telephone book looking for names of high school friends. Where would we stay? I had very little money, no job, and two small children. Thoughts of being homeless and living out of the car scared me almost as much as the war had.

I was fortunate when I found the telephone number of an old high school buddy. When we were growing up, he had dated and eventually married the girl that lived next door to my parents. I called him, and he and his wife told me to bring the kids over and stay with them until I could get a job and place to live.

Over the next several weeks, I managed to get another job working in finance. I was hired as the collection manager for a savings and loan company. Once again, I had come full circle and was doing what I had done immediately after the war. I did not want to repeat the mistakes I had made then. I would be more sympathetic toward people's problems. I would not let my anger control me again.

Eventually, I changed jobs trying to get ahead in life. I had begun teaching myself computer programming in the final months of my Army service and was trying to break into programming as a profession. I had landed a job that promised a future in that field, but it didn't work out. After two years since my discharge from the Army, I found myself out of work again.

My parents had moved back to Winchester, Virginia where I was born. My stepfather had retired, and my mother wanted to return to her own roots. I had no choice, I had to call them and ask for their help.

I hadn't spoken to my mother for two years, but she was very pleasant and told us to pack our things and move in with them. That lasted exactly one day. She could not stand to have us in the same house with her. She instructed my father to give me as much money as I needed to move out and get a house of my own and to keep giving me money until I found a job.

My job search took me back to banking and back to another job in bill collecting – full circle again, when would it end? This time I stuck with it. By now, Linda and I had divorced. I got custody of both children, but my youngest made the decision on her own to go live with her mother. Eventually,

I signed papers to let her new stepfather adopt her, while I continued to raise my older daughter on my own.

The months at the bank quickly turned into years. I eventually showed the bank what I could do with a computer, and I worked my way up to Assistant Vice President and Regional Compliance Officer. Through my programming efforts, I was able to get out of the bill collecting business for good.

In July, 1988, I was reading the local newspaper when I saw a picture of some Vietnam Veterans holding up the familiar POW flag. The article said that they were convoying to Washington, DC from Oregon and were to march in the parade on the Fourth of July. They invited any local veterans to join them. They were staying at a campground along the Shenandoah River.

*Vietnam Vet Convoy from Oregon to DC, courtesy Winchester Star*

I looked up the telephone number of the campground and decided to give them a call. I spoke with one of the vets and told him I was a Vietnam Veteran also and wished to join them. He told me to meet them out on Route 7 at 7:00 a.m. on the Fourth of July.

That morning, I put on some old camouflage Army fatigues and pinned my medals to my chest. On my right shoulder sleeve, I wore the insignia patch of the 3$^{rd}$ Marine Division. (It was customary in the Army to wear the patch of your combat unit on the right shoulder sleeve.)

At 7:00 a.m., I sat in my car on Route 7 waiting for the convoy to pass me. A few minutes later they did, and I followed them into Washington, DC. When we arrived on Constitution Avenue, a police officer directed us to a side street where there was a parking lot designated for us.

I parked my car and got out. Another car pulled in next to mine and a fellow and his wife got out. He looked over at me and saw the 3$^{rd}$ Marine Division patch on my right shoulder.

"Hey, you were in 3$^{rd}$ Marines? So was I." he said.

"Really, what unit were you in?"

"One three."

"I was in one three. When were you there?" I asked.

"1967 to 1968."

"I was there from 1968 to 1969!"

I walked over to his car and he reached inside and brought out a photo album, opening it to the first page.

"Do you recognize any of these men?" he asked.

I couldn't believe my eyes. There, on the first page of his album was a familiar face, the man who had trained me to be a one four man.

"Yes, that's Ralph Gordon!"

The man I was talking to was Tom Lang. Our paths had never crossed, but Tom and I had been in the same battalion. Although he arrived in Vietnam six months before me, he had been through some of the same battles as I, such as Dai Do, Lai An, and Mutter's Ridge. Tom was the company commander's radio operator while I was a tactical air controlman. We were never in the same company at the same time, though.

For the remainder of the day, Tom and I talked about our experiences in Vietnam. He mentioned some things that I had almost forgotten, and we both found that some of our memories of the war were fading.

That afternoon a large group of us, all Vietnam Veterans, marched in the parade down Constitution Avenue. It had been 20 years to the day that I had fought in the second battle in a village called Lai An. The emotions of that day swept over me in waves as we received a standing ovation all the way down Constitution Avenue. I had once again come full circle.

At the end of the parade route, we all gathered at the Wall – the Vietnam Memorial. I had heard about the Wall but had never visited it. I wiped the tears from my eyes as I looked up Corporal Colin Bach's name and found it on panel 40W, line 017. It was an emotional day for all of us.

After twenty years of turmoil and emotional struggle to put the war behind me, I was finally proud again that I was once a Marine. The words that so often echoed in my mind, "One four man up!" would be an everlasting memory but no longer a nightmare. My struggle to survive the war itself, as well as the war within me, was finally coming to an end. That day was one of the best days in my entire life and one that I will never forget.

*Tom Lang and Bob Hunt – July 4, 1988*

# AFTERWARD

Marching in the parade in Washington, DC on the Fourth of July was the beginning of the healing of emotional wounds I had suffered after serving one year in combat in Vietnam. So much of my life had been defined and affected by that single year. It had been so difficult to give meaning to my survival and to put the war behind me.

I had suffered horrible Post Traumatic Stress Disorder that still surfaces now and then. Although the dreams of that day in the DMZ are no longer horrifying, at least once a year I dream I am back in Vietnam watching artillery impact in the distance. I feel safe in my dreams now. There is no more fear of death, only the reminder of past experiences.

When I returned home after the parade, I reflected on my tour of duty and was inspired to start writing a book about those experiences. I wanted to preserve the memories for the sake of my children. I wanted them to know what war had done to their father and how it had affected his life so when they had children of their own, they would think seriously about sending them off to war. However, I also wanted my children to feel pride for my service and accomplishments.

In 1989, I tried to organize a group of Vietnam veterans to march in the Winchester Apple Blossom parade. I made application with the parade officials to put the group in the parade, but my request was denied. On the opening day of the parade, my picture appeared on the front page of the Winchester Star with the headlines, "Vietnam Vets Can't Get in Festival Parade."

I couldn't believe that after 20 years, I was still being treated this way. The irony of it all was that the president of the festival was a Vietnam veteran himself. In a discussion with him, he stated that if he let us march, he would have to let the Ku Klux Klan march, because we were not an organized unit. The following year, after the Persian Gulf War broke out, he begged me to be in his parade and ride on a float that would have a veteran from each foreign war represented – World War II, Korea and Vietnam. I strongly refused the offer.

After the parade interview I did with the newspaper, a reporter approached me about doing another article for the paper. When the first reporter visited my house, she saw a number of needle art pieces hanging on the wall. I had taken up counted cross stitch years ago as a way to meditate and reflect on my experiences in Vietnam. I granted the interview; and, weeks later an article appeared on the front page of the area section titled "Decorated Veteran – Cross Stitcher."

In the year that followed, I worked diligently on my book. At that time the title was "Once a Marine. " I tried to get it published but was unsuccessful. It sat on a shelf for another 20 years. It collected dust but was not forgotten.

Eventually I remarried, and now I enjoy the company of a loving wife, Peggy. My children are grown and my oldest daughter has a daughter of her own. I tried several times to make amends with my mother but never succeeded. Her mental illnesses stood in the way, and both Peggy and I had to endure additional abusiveness from her. She has since passed away from dementia.

My efforts in computer programming eventually paid off, and I was able to secure a job as an internet programmer. At the peak of that career, I was the lead programmer for television personality, Martha Stewart. I had seven programmers working under me.

Every skill that I have learned, I have taught myself. The incident at Old Dominion University kept me from ever attending college again. I sometimes wonder what I might have become had I pursued a college degree instead of going to Vietnam.

My sister, Pam, and I have become very close over the years. Often we've sat and talked about our mother and the various things she did to us over the years. Neither of us could ever accept my mother's mental illnesses, and the only way we were ever able to live with it was to distance ourselves from her.

In 1989, I took up a new hobby, building wooden model ships. I have always liked to make things with my hands. As far back as I can remember, I've built models of one kind or another. At the time, I was visiting a local hobby shop on a routine basis buying plastic models of World War II aircraft. When I told the shop owner that I might like to try my hand at model ships, he laughed and told me I couldn't do it, it was too difficult.

That was 19 years ago; and today Peggy and I own our own business, Lauck Street Shipyard LLC. We design and produce our own line of historic model ship kits. Like programming, I taught myself how to build these wonderful models. Also, the Winchester Star newspaper did another article about me and my new business when it first started up.

Over the years I saw how poorly the kits on the market were produced. The quality of the wood was poor, the instructions were poor, the designs were poor and often not historically correct. So when I got laid off from my job as a computer programmer at Susquehanna Technologies just months after 9/11, I decided that I could do better than those big companies producing model ship kits. I taught myself how to use AutoCAD and eventually learned how to take CAD drawings and apply them to computer controlled machinery (CNC mills).

Peggy has always supported my hobby and is a 50/50 partner in the business. She too spends much of her time in the production of our kits. We pride ourselves in producing the best quality model ship kits on the market. It's a small niche market, but I have gained the respect and admiration of those who love to build such models. We have shipped our kits around the world. We have a website where customers can purchase our products, and ship modelers can exchange questions and share modeling experiences with one another (http://www.lauckstreetshipyard.com).

The war in Vietnam is 40 years behind me now, but it will always be a part of me until the day I die. With Peggy's help, I have taken that original book written 20 years ago and have refined and rewritten it. I obtained unit chronologies from the Marine Corps under the Freedom of Information Act. These unclassified documents have helped me tell my story with facts that are well documented. I was elated to read these papers and find references to the many events I encountered during my tour. They helped to solidify in my own mind that my memories were real, that these events really did happen to me, and that they happened exactly as I remembered them.

*Robert E. Hunt, 1967, USMC*